THE GENERAL CUSTER STORY

THE TRUE STORY OF THE BATTLE
OF THE LITTLE BIG HORN

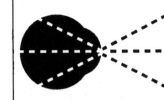

This Large Print Book carries the
Seal of Approval of N.A.V.H.

THE
GENERAL CUSTER
STORY

THE TRUE STORY OF THE BATTLE
OF THE LITTLE BIG HORN

Lauran Paine

G.K. Hall & Co.
Thorndike, Maine

Published in 1996 by arrangement with Golden West Literary Agency.

G.K. Hall Large Print Western Collection.

The text of this Large Print edition is unabridged.
Other aspects of the book may vary from the original edition.

Set in 16 pt. Bookman Old Style by Warren S. Doersam.

Printed in the United States on permanent paper.

Library of Congress Cataloging in Publication Data

Paine, Lauran.
   The General Custer story : the true story of the Battle of the Little Big Horn / by Lauran Paine. — Large print ed.
     p.   cm.
   ISBN 0-7838-1852-1 (lg. print : hc)
   1. Custer, George Armstrong, 1839–1876. 2. Little Bighorn, Battle of the, Mont., 1876. I. Title.
   [E83.876.P25 1996]
   973.8′2—dc20   96-20237

For . . .

Mita kola wasicum waste:
Che Maza —

REG BATCHELOR

Chapter One

AT the Fort Laramie peace conference, 6th November, 1868, the United States signed a treaty with the Sioux Nation in admission of defeat.

Under formidable Oglala Sioux spokesman Red Cloud, the Indians had won a smashing victory over the U.S. Army to become the only foe of the United States to meet its army upon American soil, defeat it and dictate the terms for peace.

The treaty specified that Indian land was to remain the property of the redmen for "as long as the grass shall grow. . . ." American forts were to be dismantled or destroyed, white settlers ordered out of Indian country, railroad tracks taken up, emigrant roads closed and a constabulary force stationed along the frontier to enforce compliance.

Theoretically the Northwestern Indian wars were at an end, and in fact a peace-of-sorts did exist for a time, but meanwhile the westering tide of emigration stalled behind the frontier posts, settlers filled up the villages and settlements and more came every day. Inevitably there were violations of the border. White men crossed into Indian-dom without sanction, hunted and explored. Some were caught and killed, others were not. Occasionally in retaliation but just as often in accordance with milleniums of environmental aggressiveness the Indians raided and killed outside their boundaries. No matter how distant a wagon-train bivouaced from the line of demarcation the imminence of sudden attack was for ever a threat. It was an uneasy and perhaps an unnatural peace that existed. It was not popular with the soldiers detailed to its enforcement; it was even less popular with the whites who had crossed a continent under the most trying of circumstances only to be stopped at the threshold of a new and rich life by hordes of aborigines in red blankets brandishing lances and muskets. Still, it existed, if not in the hearts of men then at least on a solemnly subscribed-to piece of paper.

During the severe winter of 1873 a party of soldiers and explorers lay idle at Fort Abraham Lincoln. There were hardships; an officer's baby died, was buried in a crate lined with old clothing. There was no chaplain to pray over the icy grave. Frequently rations were short, the result of peculations involving the President of the United States' brother, Orville Grant. The Indians were troublesome, strong in numbers, restless, quite antagonistic. Their treaty was now five years old.

The next spring, 1874, a lieutenant-colonel at Fort Abraham Lincoln named George Armstrong Custer, second in command of the 7th Regiment of Cavalry, led an exploring party into Indiandom in violation of the 1868 treaty.

By 8th July he was exploring the Short Pine Hills area of what is now South Dakota. By the 17th he was leading a strong party in a circuitous sortie which lasted until the 27th or 28th, when he returned to the base camp. Here his party was suprised by a Sioux hunting party. There were anxious moments until the Indians withdrew. This happened at Castle Creek.

Three days later Colonel Custer, Charley Reynolds, several prospectors and Professor Donaldson, all civilians except Custer, went on a side-trip to where present-day Edgemont is, and flamboyantly egotistical, exaggeratingly articulate and rarely correct Custer was so elated at the showings of fine gold the prospectors found that he wrote there was "gold from the grass roots down".

The expedition then moved northward and spent an aggravating week trying to find a passage to Bear Butte for the wagons. They went up Middle Box Elder to Hay Creek, over to Little Elk, then back to Box

Elder and down to Bogus Jim Creek. Still thwarted they groped along a dark canyon until they came to Black Hawk. From there they struck out over Elk Creek Gap, made a camp southeast of Bear Butte from which they explored the locality ahorseback. Concluding eventually that access to Bear Butte with wagons was impractical, they broke camp, returned southward to the Cave Hills and Short Pine country were they remained until 19th August, 1874.

This exploration under the aegis of Colonel Custer, so little known today, was ironic. After 8th July the Custer party was in violation of a treaty whites, especially army officers, were bound to honour. The hostilities which resulted from Custer's excited dispatch about the finding of gold, did not end until the man who had aroused the greed in every settler's heart, was dead; a victim of the storm he had himself unleashed. But there was also tragedy, for he was leading several hundred others when the end came; they died with him.

The Fort Laramie Treaty was now six years old, in defiance settlers had dared to cross the line in numbers. Some had even established homes and ranches on the fringe of Indiandom. Unanimous white opinion condemned the borderline, the soldiers who patrolled it reluctantly, the redskins beyond who did not deserve to own such an empire, and the politicians who had originally agreed to its establishment. Government authorities could ignore the clamour until it became great enough, which it did after the discovery of gold by Custer's party in 1874. After that it would have taken an Army Corps to keep the violaters from slipping over the line. No such force was available and the soldiers who were on hand, harassed, abused, de-moralised, had little reason to strive, for only the newest recruits among them had not seen white corpses after Indian raids, or had not lost a companion during the intermittent battles.

Gold brought hundreds of eager people, but it was not gold that caused the final resumption of hostilities. It helped be-cause it swelled settler-ranks with newcom-ers, but other factors were vastly more important. Indian raiding into U.S. territory increased as the white population grew. Fighting spread, involved whole settlements and whole tribes. Finally, Senator Benton's "Manifest Destiny" — the rolling tide of empire — which could not be halted, had come to exert a pressure, an articulate and militant pressure that mounted for six years until no hypothetical line, invisible, drawn on paper, could hold it back. By then it was inevitable that the Fort Laramie Treaty would not be supported by the white government of Washington, and while the subsequent invasion of Indiandom was not authorised, it was not discouraged either.

The Indian defence of their treaty lands was swift and savage. As though in anticipation of the Federal Government's failure to honour its commitment, warriors hurled themselves upon the white invaders. When no great effort was made by the white soldiers to restrain settlers, Indian council fires burnt late, zealots demanded the taking up of the hatchet. Others did not await but carried war to every wagon-train, every lone miner, every party, large or small, found in Indiandom. The frontier flamed, the Army had its hands full and a state of war existed. By dividing its force the Army pursued raiding parties over the line in U.S. territory, and alternatively detailed detachments to protect the settlers pouring into Indiandom — the same people it had only a short while before prohibited from crossing the line. As soon as American soldiers were seen over the line the Indians retaliated without restriction or reservation with the normal consequence that warfare was declared to exist by both sides and the Fort Laramie Treaty was scrapped. The fighting which followed was not to cease for nearly a quarter of a century, and attempts at reconciliation and appeasement were negligible. Inspired by old Red Cloud's earlier triumphs the Indians were well-nigh unbeatable. So-called "tame" or Reservation Indians swarmed to the camps of the hostiles. Many of these brought with them the latest in firearms, repeating rifles and carbines. These were never in abundance however and for the most part the Sioux and their Northern Cheyenne allies were armed with bows, lances, knives and hatchets, with an occasional smoothbore musket.

Indian defection had more than the invasion to spark it for after the Fort Laramie Treaty the Federal Government had been lax in making good upon its promises. Before Custer found gold, tribute allotments had been tardy, the food sent to the Indians was very poor in quality and rarely enough in quantity. This might not have resulted in anything overt except that through agreement Indian hunting parties had been restricted in movement, their personal freedom sharply curtailed. It was therefore extremely difficult for the redmen to augment their need for food without violating the treaty they were determined to uphold. But hunger is a powerful factor, and even without it the government's policy of attempting to make over in a matter of months, nomads who for tens of thousands of years had been free-rovers, hunters, the personifications of independence, was bound to fail utterly and dismally. The

Sioux and Northern Cheyenne had a fierce and warlike heritage, they reverted to this when the American soldiers violated the border of their treaty lands, believing fully and without qualification that what they did was absolutely right and justified — which it was.

They watched the invaders come from a hundred hilltops and there was great bitterness for the U.S. Government had not even bothered to repudiate the treaty of 1868 — or the treaties of 1850 or 1851 either. The deepest knowledge of injustice motivated them. Their ferocity was so intense, their courage and fury so relentless it appeared to the emigrants that nothing could equal the formidable foe they met in the Northwestern uplands. Legends of Indian prowess grew and spread. Back in the States the old story of Indians ten feet tall shooting arrows that could penetrate an ox's carcass and kill five chickens on the far side, were resurrected.

Disaster piled upon disaster. Emigrants with the will to live and very little else were reduced to wolf-worried carcasses. There was a compensating factor without which the conquest of the West would have cost more and been delayed many years: Most of the men who crossed the Plains in the late 'sixties had been well trained in arms and the tactics of warfare, Federal or Confederate; they were capable of defending themselves providing they had warning of attack. It was the lack of warning which accounted for the many massacres — the Indian strategy was based upon stealth — rather than any general inability to fight.

The War Department had not forgot its defeat at the hands of Red Cloud. It could not risk a repetition. Public rancour abetted by the fact that the United States had no other foe to fight as had been the case in 1860-65, encouraged the marshalling of an overwhelming host to be used in crushing the Indians. No one expected the Army to be beaten in the 1870's; it had thousands of veterans, Gatling guns, repeating rifles and wheeled-artillery. It had war-proven tactics and war-tempered generals. These latter were not, as in the cases of Generals George Crook and Oliver Otis Howard, exemplary soldiers against an equal foe, but against Indians they were considered adequate. Time would give them the ultimate triumph but not many victories in the field, and while they made plans the Indians continued to raid and slaughter.

The Army's history of defeat at Indian hands stemmed from one factor. Manoeuvring so as to compel the redmen to stand and fight consumed months of time, required serpentine wagon-trains of supplies, and was never successful, yet it was inflexibly the policy of officers in the field, and this was particularly ironic for it had been by emulating the Indian tactic of striking and running, of employing every means of stealth and covert, that the Americans had triumphed over the formally aligned red-coated ranks of George III slightly less than one hundred years earlier, achieving through simulation America's independence from Britain. Indians did not fight unless the moment was auspicious for them. They chose not only the terrain but the time. They fought battles by simply appearing out of nowhere and bursting upon the enemy, catching him unprepared, fighting savagely, then fading away. This idiosyncrasy might occur where there was no particular reason for a battle at all, or again it might happen where it was thought likely Indians *would* attack. The uncertainty, plus the generally unknown, unexplored areas of the Northwest, made this type of warfare especially unpopular with the U.S. Army and its some-time allies, the emigrants. It also accounted for most of the defeats the whites suffered.

The empire of the Sioux and their allies was known to be of immeasurable depth. The Army was further hampered by unauthenticated accounts of exploration from various sources — drunk and sober — with as many variations as the weather.

In time a few dependable scouts would be found reliable but by that time there would also be innumerable graves and defeats attesting to earlier inaccuracies. Pursuit of raiders was difficult too; if the hostiles' "medicine" indicated a move was wise, a village of a thousand Indians could be trailing over the landscape beneath a stinking dustcloud within an hour or two. Vigilant and hawk-eyed scouts could discern a soldier-column twenty miles off with the result that when the dusty, tired dragoons arrived, they found only a few obscene symbols, some rubble, and travois-tracks leading into the broken hinterland. Pursuit, by its very nature, left the soldiers liable to ambush, and in this method of combat Indians excelled. Success was frequent enough to inspire the most intrepid cavalryman with great caution. All in all Indian campaigning in the latter half of the 1800's demanded not only the most resolute determination, but also the most astute caution. It would have been difficult for the best generals, but the commanders of American forces during the Northwestern Campaigns were not the best, with one or two exceptions.

Whites and Indians were irreconcilably different in most things; in warfare the perspectives were contrary but the goal identical. Methods of achievement varied greatly. But if an edge existed it lay with the Indian. He was an unorthodox fighter but his wish was victory. In battle few taboos restrained him. He was rarely bothered by chivalries, and neither was his white opponent. Before the last shot was fired both sides had reduced their contest to the basic and savage will to triumph without consideration for niceties of any kind. And if the Army had superior numbers and firepower, these were often neutralised by the Indians' knowledge of country and his whirlwind method of fighting.

This knowledge of terrain was a powerful aid to the hostile. He knew his empire as intimately as he knew the back of his hand. The white soldier did not and therefore was obliged to rely on guides who were often Judas-Indians, 'breeds, or quite often white men who had lived among the Indians or had traded across their domain. These marginal characters ordinarily knew the country far better than they knew their own loyalties.

After years of fruitless searching and skirmishing, the Army determined to advance a policy requiring the close co-operation of its various detachments in the field with the view of forcing the hostiles to fight a final and decisive contest. Several powerful columns were to be sent into Indiandom from different directions. Each was to be strong enough to overwhelm any hostiles it found, and if the Indians fled they would find themselves faced by one of the other converging commands. Thus the Indians would be surrounded by three armies, compelled to stand, and either fight or surrender. Clearly, if the plan worked, it would put an end to the Indian wars, which in turn would permit the resumption of immigration resulting in the ultimate settlement of the West. The strategy was sound and it would work in the end because there were more soldiers than Indians, but before the victorious finalé America would be presented with two thoroughly unexpected results: A hero over whose grave has raged the most heated controversy for nearly a hundred years, and a battle which has had more written about it than any other single combat in American history; Colonel Custer and the Battle of the Little Bighorn.

In compliance with orders emanating from the Chicago offices of General Phil Sheridan, Commander of the Department of the West, Brigadier General Alfred H. Terry was to proceed west from Fort Abraham Lincoln, forming one arm of the strategic pincers. Under his command was the ill-fated 7th Regiment of Cavalry under Colonel Sturgis, whose immediate subordinate was brevet Major-General, Colonel

George Armstrong Custer, a horse-faced egocentric who had achieved no small measure of notoriety during the Civil War.

The second arm of the invasion host was to proceed east into Indiandom from Fort Ellis in Montana under Colonel Gibbon, while the third striking force under General George Crook was to march from the north, or North Platte River country, where its headquarters were at Fort Fetterman. The point of juncture was to be somewhere within the landmasses between the Powder River and the Bighorn Mountains. It was decided that in order to complete the campaign before fall, 1876, co-ordinated movements should begin as soon as the weather permitted. Accordingly General Crook left Fort Fetterman in March with the mercury standing at a disagreeable thirty degrees below zero. The day Crook left Fetterman a raging blizzard struck. His van of fifteen companies of cavalry broke trail for five companies of infantry. Total force: One thousand and two men, forty-seven officers.

Also accompanying General Crook were guides Louis Richards and Baptiste Pourier; packers, teamsters, and several unwelcome newspapermen. Later, at Clear Creek, he acquired a band of sixty-five hard-bitten prospectors. Among his wheeled conveyances he also had several wagon-guns.

While Crook's column was battling the elements Colonel Gibbon left Fort Ellis in April with somewhat better weather and marched eastward to prevent hostiles from crossing the Yellowstone River. His force numbered roughly four hundred men.

Meanwhile General Alfred Terry held a review at Fort Abraham Lincoln then took the trail 7th May, 1876, and not many weeks afterwards advance elements of his command encountered scouts from Gibbon's column. Exactly two days and one month after he had left Fort Lincoln his force and the command of Gibbon met and made a joint bivouac. In effect they had completed a tactical sweep which could be considered as having erected a hypothetical barrier against roving Indian bands, but this could be implemented in conjuncture with Crook only providing they kept on the move. In fact it was imperative they avoid delay for each coordinating column was operating according to a strict timetable.

General Crook, moving northward, received word 8th June that a strong war-party of Shoshoni allies would shortly join him. He went into camp and to his astonishment, on the 9th, he was attacked by a formidable party of Sioux and Cheyennes. The attack was launched without warning from the surrounding hills and resulted in two deaths and several injuries.

21

The hostiles were driven off and Crook moved his camp to a spot less susceptible to sudden attack.

Crook was made cautious; obviously the enemy was in the area in considerable force. He had no idea where Terry and Gibbon were. While in camp awaiting the Shoshonis he was pleased to welcome one hundred and seventy-six Crow Indian allies who came up with three white scouts. This occurred on the 14th. The Crows were traditional foemen of both the Cheyennes and Sioux. Along with modern guns the Crows brought news. Gibbon, they said, was camped some distance away on the Tongue River. Both had moved by the time the Crows offered this intelligence to General Crook but it gave him a general idea where Gibbon was.

The evening of the 14th, the same day the Crows arrived, eighty-six Shoshonis rode in accompanied by three shaggy Texans. General Crook's force now numbered approximately thirteen hundred effectives.

With an idea where Gibbon was, and perhaps Terry as well, plus some notion of the whereabouts of the ellusive enemy, Crook decided to seek the hostiles in the vicinity of the Tongue River. He accordingly ordered that the wagons were to be left at the base camp, each cavalryman was to receive one hundred rounds of ammunition and four days' rations, and further that seventy-five picked infantrymen were to accompany the column mounted on the loose-stock. He hoped to find the Indians and defeat them, but in any case he intended to force his way through their land and affect a meeting with Gibbon on the Yellowstone.

At five in the morning of the 16th he led out. When the Tongue was reached his command followed the river downstream, or northwest, until early in the afternoon when far-ranging scouts brought back word of a fresh Indian-trail ahead. Crook's Indian allies became upset and noisy. Altering his course somewhat he encountered several small bands of buffalo. Orders had been passed that no unnecessary noise was to be made, for it was felt that the Indians they were after had as yet no idea white soldiers were close by. However, when the Crows and Shoshonis saw the buffalo they broke ranks and charged them, firing and screaming as they went. Reprimanded, the allies loaded dripping hunks of ribs, butt-meat and hump roast upon their horses, fell in at the columns' rear and rode contentedly along until camp was made on the south fork of the Rosebud. The command had covered forty miles.

Scouts were unable to locate the Indians although they tried late into the night of the 16th. Around the cooking fires there was considerable speculation as to where the hostiles could have gone. When officers expressed a wish to ascertain at least the direction they had taken a white scout offered to go seek the trail, but requested some of the allied Indians as protective companions, when they refused to go the matter was dropped.

On the other hand the hostile Indians had known of Crook's coming and had in fact left vedettes behind to watch him all day the 16th. They were just as confident of a victory over the soldiers as the latter were of a victory over them. Among the warriors Crook was pursuing were many from the reservations, well armed and with an abundance of ammunition.

Six days before sighting Crook on the 16th they had held a "big stomp" — a Sun Dance — which was "powerful medicine," and their renowned recalcitrant Sitting Bull had participated with such unusual vigour that his back and legs bothered him for two days afterwards; but he had had a vision and from this came the hostiles' belief in their present invincibility.

On the 15th the Indians had been in camp not more than twenty miles from the soldiers. There, on the Rosebud, the land was made up of hills and valleys. There was timber, great sweeps of land, arroyos and buttes which could screen five hundred tipis within a mile. Because Crook's scouts had been motivated more by prudence than aggressiveness they had never found the Indian encampment, and later, when the soldiers were seeking them, the hostiles had broken this camp and crossed the divide between the Little Bighorn and the Rosebud, and made their next camp beside a little tributary waterway which would soon be named Reno Creek. At this camp a warrior died. After Sioux custom, when not in an area where they could build a burial platform, or find a tree to lash the corpse into, or a deep, hidden crevice, the Indians laid their dead warrior out in his finest attire within his own tipi and left him there. Mourners would wail and inflict injuries upon themselves for several days, normally, while the rest of the band moved on.

But General Crook did not know that this was a particularly large band; in fact several villages travelling together which could put over two thousand warriors into the field against him. Moreover, unbeknownst to him but strongly in his favour, despite Sitting Bull's vision and their general warlikeness, the Indians were divided among themselves. One clique of spokesmen was for all-out war while another equally strong division of the band felt that no concerted action should be taken as yet. In the end this latter group modified their conviction by saying that if the tribesmen felt impelled in large measure to attack the invaders, then only the volunteer warriors should be permitted to go; all others should remain behind to protect the village.

This met with general approval, but again, as has been stressed elsewhere, Indian warriors fought as individuals; upon the eve of battle some would oversleep or simply change their minds and decide against going out to battle. Others might spend interminable lengths of time making up their warrior-toilet or communing with spirits, while close by a fierce battle might bc in progress. Conversely, the most eager and blood-thirsty warriors might charge an enemy single-handed, going to certain death of course but more important, giving an enemy warning of impending attack. The warrior-societies — the *akicitas* — were therefore compelled to patrol the camps constantly, not only when the tribe was on the warpath, but during the hunt and even while at peace in camp. Each *akicita* acted in this police capacity on certain days and no one could disobey them upon pain of banishment or death.

While in their Dead Warrior encampment, during the course of considerable disagreement among themselves which was eventually resolved by the expedient of permitting volunteers to attack Crook's soldiers, it was stated that no warrior could go out to fight except under the aegis of the ruling *akicita*. In this way the soldiers might be fallen upon without warning. A thousand or so warriors adorned themselves for battle, painted their "medicine" symbols upon themselves and their horses and rode quietly through the darkness towards Crook's camp. The policing *akicita* was able to restrain most of the strong-heartbucks but Sitting Bull and a small party managed to slip away. However this latter band was unable to make very good time in the darkness and did not arrive upon the slopes overlooking Crook's camp until sunup, at which time the balance of the war-party also arrived. Sioux leaders were Kicking Bear and Crazy Horse; Northern Cheyenne leaders were Little Hawk and lesser war-chieftains.

A careful reconnaissance was made after which it was decided to withdraw to a particularly attractive ambushing spot. The route of General Crook was surmised correctly prior to the withdrawal, but again, the waiting was odious and the *akicita* had a difficult time preventing premature and individual charges. The majority of the warriors spent the time completing their prayers, reasserting their dominance, and in general watching the river from behind the hill which screened them.

General Crook was totally ignorant of what was awaiting him. An experienced Indian fighter who had smashed the Apaches and would crush them again, he now started out along the river with his companies closed up in good marching and defensive order. He ordered the Crows and Shoshonis out ahead as scouts and skirmishers. It was his intention to follow the tracks his men had found the day before to the Indian village. Like nearly all Army officers of his time he believed firmly that the surest way to whip Indians was to find their villages, destroy them utterly; minimise the means of hostiles to wage war. But in this case if General Crook's knowledge of the country was limited, it is hard to believe that his scouts and allies had not been over this same land before. In any case it seems incredible that one thousand warriors could hide so well, in the face of Crook's scouts and skirmishers, that they would go undetected. This is what happened and General Crook with two hundred and fifty-one Crows, Shoshonis, and white scouts searching the terrain ahead of his column, marched to an object-lesson many had learnt before him, and George Armstrong Custer would learn after him: The Indians were not trying to run away any more.

Disparity was marked. Crook outnumbered his foemen. His men were indisputably better armed, for while many Indians had good weapons not all did. On the other hand among the hostiles were many veteran warriors who could darken the sky with arrows. It was not uncommon for fighting Indians to be able to keep five and six arrows in flight at the same time. Their aim and accuracy was equal; at infighting a good bowman was not inferior to a pistol-wielding soldier. Crook had ordnance, of course, but to offset this somewhat the Indians had the element of surprise, and Crook did not make good use of his guns. Furthermore, he believed right up to the moment the first yell was raised that the hostiles which he knew were somewhere ahead, were neither in sufficient force, nor close enough, to pose an immediate or lasting threat. Like Gibbon and Terry, in fact because it was mandatory that no additional defeats be met with, each of the three converging armies was deliberately stronger than was customary, and each commander was confident he could deal conclusively with any Indians which attacked him, or which he attacked. But again, General Crook's liaison was faulty; no report arrived even warning of the possibility of hostiles ahead.

At Rosebud Canyon Crook hesitated. The place was a natural ambuscade. He ordered a thorough scout made before moving on. The horses were watered and a brief halt called at a large bend in the river. The day was sparkling clear and warm. A solitary gunshot broke the stillness. The soldiers leapt up. A careening party of Crow scouts raced towards them from the direction of a low hill. The Indians were shouting and waving their weapons. As the soldiers moved forward to meet them the ridge of the hill behind the Crows came to life with a vividly arrayed host of hostiles who raised the yell and hurled themselves down the near slope directly at Crook's column.

The soldiers, caught off guard, were not as unprepared as they might have been, for that second of warning had been enough for most to reach their arms. They met the Sioux and Cheyenne charge without breaking. The warriors broke along their front and veered off. Immediately General Crook ordered a counter-charge. A bugle sounded, the soldiers mounted and went after the hostiles. The following portrayal by a participant of this fight leaves little to be imagined:

". . . The Indians proved then and there that they were the best cavalry soldiers on earth. In charging up towards us they exposed little of their person, hanging on with one arm around the neck and one leg over the horse, firing and lancing from underneath the horse's neck, so that there was no part of an Indian at which we could aim.

"Their shouting and personal appearance was so hideous that it terrified the horses more than our men and rendered them almost uncontrollable before we dismounted and placed them behind the rocks.

"The Indians came not in a line but in flocks or herds like the buffalo, and they piled in upon us until I think there must have been one thousand or fifteen hundred in our immediate front, but they refused to fight when they found us secured behind the rocks, and bore off to our left. . . ."

On Crook's left were the units under Colonels Henry and Royal, as well as the Crows and Shoshonis under Lieutenant Bourke. Crook's allied Indians were greatly aggravated by so many screaming Sioux and Cheyennes who, upon seeing Indians fighting with tlie soldiers, turned their ferocity on them with a sustained charge and a maniacal fury, which, while it did not succeed in routing the Crows or Shoshonis, made a deep impression upon them and they would leave as soon as they thought it safe to do so.

In the course of the hostile attack upon the "tame" Indians there was much hand-to-hand fighting which prevented the soldiers from aiding their allies out of fear of shooting the wrong Indians. During this phase of the battle Colonel Henry was wounded and nearly captured alive. Soldiers rallied to the aid of their savage allies and secured the Colonel's release from his captors but nothing, it seemed, could check the hostiles' fury.

The civilians with Crook, particularly the sixty-five miners whose position was in the centre of the line, could do little beyond sniping until the hostiles were beaten back from the left. But, because Crook's centre where the miners lay, protruded past both flanks, the men there had an unequalled view of the battlefield, and it was due to their marksmanship that the initial phase of the fighting ended without Crook's line being breached. Indian reserves storming up to aid their companions on the left, were halted by a devastating fire from the miners; then, without sustaining force, the hostiles were forced back and the men in the centre poured volley after volley into the retreating warriors. The reinforcements had been checked, the charge repulsed, and the hostiles drew off.

General Crook's men remained in position and the hostiles returned again and again, hammering incessantly at the line unmindful of casualties. This variety of combat was unexpected; it was Indian custom to strike and flee, rarely indeed did they launch sustained attacks. Mounted warriors on wounded or fear-maddened mounts rode over the defenders time and again, but the lines did not give way. In some instances the attackers were able to isolate little pockets of soldiers or friendlies and when these would not be vanquished the hostiles broke off and threw themselves against the main line again and again. General Crook who had triumphed over the wily and vicious Apaches learnt the difference between Desert and Plains Indians, on the Rosebud. If Crazy Horse and Little Hawk had been able to breach his line a massacre equal to that which occurred eight days later on the Little Bighorn would have pre-dated the destiny of Custer's 7th Cavalry.

When the battle's intensity seemed to slacken General Crook detached eight companies of cavalry to hasten down the canyon, seek and attack the hostile village. It was Crook's opinion that so many warriors must mean a village close by. Oddly, however, very few hostiles followed the troopers, which indicated that no village was near. More significantly from the hostile viewpoint, Crook had divided his command.

Crook meant to follow after the eight companies as soon as he could extricate himself but this was impossible for as soon as they saw his detachment leave the hostiles mounted a new and vigorous assault all along his line. So fierce and determined were the renewed attacks Crook was obliged to send a courier after the detachment ordering it to return at once.

In returning the eight companies made a wide detour of the field, approached it from a new direction in order to negate the possibility of an ambush, and in so doing inadvertently gave General Crook invaluable aid. The hostiles, sighting the charging column coming up mistook it for reinforcements and broke off the battle, withdrew beyond range and watched the "newcomers" ride up. By then it was two o'clock in the afternoon and the battle had lasted nearly four hours. Now it was ended. The hostiles rode up the hill and sat their horses watching the soldiers and friendlies. The latter mounted their horses and rode up and down howling insults and challenges which were occasionally answered but no further fighting occurred.

The hostiles had exhausted not only their ammunition but their mounts. They had not lost many men, were able to reclaim most of the bodies before riding off leaving Crook in command of the field.

General Crook posted a strong guard and went into bivouac. He subsequently reported that he had lost only ten men killed and twenty-one wounded. Off-setting this the Crows and Shoshonis had thirteen hostile scalps. Participant and noted scout Frank Grouard said Crook lost twenty-eight killed and fifty-seven wounded while Lieutenant Bourke said a total of fifty-seven were killed and wounded. Indian losses in this battle as in others, varied according to authorities. They lost approximately eleven killed and three wounded. After dark burial parties wrapped each of Crook's casualties in a blanket and buried them on the banks of the Rosebud. Horses were led back and forth over the graves to obliterate all signs. The Indians who had fallen too close to the firing line to be salvaged by their companions were scalped and left lying.

General Crook then retreated towards his base camp carrying the wounded on travois. In bivouac the night of the 18th on the Tongue River the Crows left, waiting until full darkness was down to begin their exodus from Sioux country. Early on the 19th of June, 1876, Crook's command arrived back at the base camp on Goose Creek where "General Crook and all of us made very brief reports of tlie fighting, having little pride in our accomplishment."

This was the famous Battle of the Rosebud. It was not the first time hostile Indians had forced the course of a battle against the soldiers but it most certainly was one of the most rigorously prosecuted Indian fights General Crook had ever participated in. He did not know about the Bull's vision of course, nor had he any inkling he was opposed by one of the Sioux' most formidable war-leaders. But he *did* know from no little experience that Indians normally fought so fiercely only in defence of their villages. He had many precedents to foster his by no means rare belief that Indians would not stand and fight; Conner's attack upon the villages at the Bear and Tongue Rivers, Reynolds' attack on the Powder and Custer's attack of Black Kettle's village on the Washita. Nevertheless he had found and faced an altogether different brand of fanaticism on the Rosebud, and afterwards he was content to remain in camp at Goose Creek, and by the time General Sheridan in Chicago learnt of his defeat on the Rosebud it was too late to warn General Terry; he was well beyond the nearest telegraph line, deep in country where dispatch riders were swallowed up and never heard from again.

After their victory on the Rosebud the hostiles held their customary victory celebration — not always justified — and went hunting. Messengers were sent to other bands with news of the great triumph over Crook — who was called Grey Fox — and this had the effect of drawing the bands closer together. White reaction was understandably different. The Army did not claim a victory on the Rosebud although the Indians withdrew first and George Crook's meagre pinch of glory which should have arisen from his good defence was swept away by recriminations, court martials, and severe censuring. The factor for which he may have deserved censure was his handling of the artillery; it was not used effectively nor in time.

Striking their camp on Medicine Dance Creek (Reno Creek) the Indians straggled southward over the broken country and streamed down into Little Bighorn Valley. They made a camp on the east bank of the Little Bighorn River, the Cheyennes, as was the custom, a little way up-river from the Sioux. Game was plentiful. There was ample forage for their large horse herd. Reservation Indians drifted in singly and in small parties. They stayed at this camp until the 24th of June because the hunting was good and the squaws wished to exploit the opportunity to lay in as much winter stores as they could. The scouts trailing Crook's column sent back reports. The soldiers were withdrawing still farther southward. There were many dances and ceremonials officially celebrating the victory of the Rosebud.

The trickle of "tame" or reservation Indians, grew with each passing day. They had heard of Crook's defeat before the whites had; had used the interval to acquire all the ammunition they could get before "jumping the line" and joining their compatriots. The singular fact that Indian Agents in charge of reservations invariably minimised the number of Indians who defected accounted in no small degree for the great disparity in the estimated number of hostiles, and the actual number.

The Shoshonis now left Crook as the Crows had. Feeling these losses Crook asked for additional reinforcements. About this time Eastern newspapers undertook to upbraid the Army for its current failure in the face of its previous confidence and reiteration that the Sioux War would be a strictly local and swift campaign which could end only one way. In the face of unpleasant notoriety General Phil Sheridan, Commander, Department of the West, prepared to make an on-the-field investigation but by the time he arrived in the theatre of action American history and Western legend had over two hundred martyrs and a conflict of testimony second to none.

A few days prior to Crook's meeting with the hostiles on the Rosebud the reinforced column under General Terry — including Gibbon's command — was scouting for hostiles. Aware the Indians were not far, considerable activity was undertaken to prevent any untoward meeting. During this lull while Terry awaited reports from his scouts and General Crook was recovering from the calamitous meeting with Crazy Horse, it would be well to fill in the time with a report on the personality and character of Lieutenant-Colonel Custer.

Born 5th December, 1839, at New Rumley, Ohio, Custer's father was a blacksmith, his mother, Maria Ward Kirkpatrick, a strong-willed Pennsylvanian. At the age of ten Custer was sent to Monroe, Michigan, to live with a half-sister. There he attended Monroe Normal School and Monroe Academy. By 1856 he was a schoolteacher back at New Rumley. In 1857 he got an appointment to the United States Military Academy at West Point where in 1861, with the Civil War raging, at the bottom of his class, he was noted as being "regardless of academic regulations."

His record caused some discussion as to whether he should be graduated or not. He was retained at the Point while more intelligent and amenable classmates went off to war, but eventually the balance fell in his favour and he was sent to join a regiment in time to participate in the Federal defeat at Bull Run — or Manassas. He subsequently served on the staffs of General

Kearny and W. F. Smith. His boldness in action at the Battle of Chickahominy brought him to the attention of General George Brinton McClellan who had him attached to his staff with the rank of captain.

In 1863 he became aide-de-camp to General Pleasanton, participated in the campaigns of Pennsylvania, Rappahannock, and central Virginia. In June, 1863, he rose to the rank of brevet Brigadier-General and distinguished himself at the head of the Michigan Cavalry at the Battle of Gettysburg.

He married Elizabeth Bacon of Monroe, Michigan, in 1864 and served with the Army of the Potomac under General Phil Sheridan. In October he was breveted major-general, youngest officer to hold that rank in the American Army since de Lafayette.

In 1864 he received the only wound acquired during the Civil War and although it was trivial, his proximity to combat is attested by the fact that he had eleven horses shot from under him.

Under Custer Michigan's 3rd Cavalry became prominent for its achievements. It captured ten thousand Confederate soldiers, seven generals, sixty-five Rebel colours and one hundred and eleven pieces of artillery, while never losing a flag nor being defeated in action. At Appomattox General Custer rode to Confederate General James Longstreet's camp and demanded his surrender. Longstreet bade Custer return to the Federal lines before he had him shot. Later, when the fighting was ended Custer was given the honour of taking the flag of truce from Confederate General Robert E. Lee. In addition he led the last Federal charge against the Rebels; against a South Carolina contingent which refused to surrender. It was also Custer who, after Lee and Grant had signed the articles of capitulation, made off with the marble-topped table upon which the historic document had been signed.

After the war Custer in fringed buckskin and flowing blond hair, rode past president-elect Ulysses S. Grant's reviewing stand without saluting, thus deepening an animosity toward Custer which Grant had acquired earlier, or during the war.

By 1866 the major-general had been cut back to the rank of lieutenant-colonel in accordance with the policy which reduced general ranks in keeping with the size of the standing army. He had been stationed in Texas and the Southwest; was for a time chief of cavalry in the Department of Texas, had attacked Cheyennes under Black Kettle on the Washita with his band playing the regimental air "Garry Owen". The Indians, although caught unprepared, rallied and fought vigorously. In order to cover his withdrawal Lieutenant-Colonel Custer ordered his rear-guard under Major Elliott to hold the Indians while the balance of the force withdrew. The defence was good; Elliott and all his men were killed. On 28th July, 1867, Custer was ordered under arrest by his Departmental Commander. In September a court martial found him guilty of seven derelictions including *disregarding orders,* deserting his command in hostile country, having enlisted men shot for minor infractions of regulations, and refusing medical aid to soldiers who were then abandoned, and who died. On 8th November, 1867, the charges and sentence were reviewed and confirmed. A Board of Review expressed dissatisfaction with the court's leniency in sentencing Custer to a reprimand and recommended he be held on charges of murder. President Grant did not intervene to support the recommendation, however, and the sentencing to a reprimand stood.

On 3rd January, 1868, Judge Adams of Leavenworth, issued a warrant for Custer's arrest on a charge of murder. This attempt to try the lieutenant-colonel before a civilian tribunal was circumvented by the Army and Colonel Custer was restored to duty.

Custer's record from 1868 until 1876 was

mediocre, then through incautious and imprudent writings and sayings he became involved in the impeachment proceedings against President Grant's Secretary of War, William W. Belknap. By then Custer was with the 7th Cavalry at Fort Abraham Lincoln. The 7th's regular commanding officer, Colonel Sturgis, was on detached service. But his son Lieutenant James G. Sturgis was with the command. Colonel Custer was one of the officers General Terry had to rely upon, and while in 1876 he was not the "boy general" of 1864 — his blond hair was thinning, he had acquired a perpetual squint — in many ways his record, so far as fighting Indians was concerned, was worthy of Terry's trust.

But Custer nearly missed his rendezvous with Destiny. In supporting the impeachment proceedings pending against William Belknap with unbecoming enthusiasm he had incurred the wrath of his superiors in the nation's capital. He was ordered relieved of command and directed to present himself at Washington as a witness at the very time the 1876 campaign against the hostiles was being organised. He wired Washington to be excused, then notified General Terry of his summons, to which Terry replied: ". . . I am sorry to have you go for I fear it will delay our movements . . . you might ask to be relieved from personal attendance without exposing yourself to any misconstructions."

Custer wrote Washington, then had a change of heart and sent the following to General Terry: "After further consideration fearing my request to be relieved from obeying the summons might be misconstrued into a desire to avoid testifying I have concluded to prefer no request to that effect."

He went to Washington and remained there until 2nd May. Meanwhile President Grant personally directed that another officer be given his command. Custer then entrained for the West without permission. When his departure came to light the War Department, President Grant, and the Army's staff, joined in sending the following telegram to General Phil Sheridan at Chicago, with orders to transmit it to General Terry at Fort Abraham Lincoln:

"The Lieutenant-General directs me to transmit to you the following telegram from the General of the Army for your information and action:

'General P. H. Sheridan, Chicago, Illinois.

I am at this moment advised that General Custer started last night for St. Paul and Fort Abraham Lincoln. He was not justified in leaving without seeing the President and myself. Please intercept him and await further orders; meantime let the expedition proceed without him.

/s/ W. T. Sherman, General'

"Should Lieutenant-Colonel Custer not be intercepted here you will take such steps as will secure his detention at St. Paul until further orders are received from higher authority.

/s/ R. C. Drum"

Custer was halted at Chicago. He immediately sent a lengthy and plausible letter to General Sherman in Washington setting forth his reasons for leaving. The nature and tone of the message reflected bewilderment and injury. It ended with his need for haste being attributable to the necessity of meeting General Terry before the expedition against the Sioux got under way.

General Sherman was slightly appeased. He directed Sheridan to permit Custer to proceed, then sent the following wire to General Terry through General Sheridan's office: ". . . Have just come from the President with orders that General Custer be allowed to rejoin his post, there to remain on duty, but not to accompany the expedition supposed to be on the point of starting against the hostile Indians under General Terry."

Custer returned to Fort Lincoln having won the battle only to lose the war. He termed it "humiliation" and threw himself upon General Terry's compassion "with tears in his eyes." Terry wired an urgent request for permission to include Custer in the expedition. This was forwarded by General Sheridan with a plea from Custer, to General Sherman. Sheridan added an acid endorsement: ". . . I am sorry Lieutenant-Colonel Custer did not manifest as much interest in staying at his post to organise and get ready his regiment and the expedition as he now does to accompany it. On a previous occasion in eighteen sixty-eight I asked executive clemency for Colonel Custer to enable him to accompany his regiment against the Indians, and I sincerely hope that if granted this time it may have sufficient effect to prevent him from again attempting to throw discredit upon his profession and his brother officers. . . ."

The amended order from General Sherman to General Terry in part: ". . . Custer's urgent request to go under your command with his regiment has been submitted to the President, who sent me word that if you want General Custer along he withdraws his objections. Advise Custer to be prudent, not to take along any newspapermen, who always make mischief, and to abstain from personalities in the future. . . ."

Conceivably Alfred Terry acquainted Custer with only the pertinent portions of this message for when he left Fort Lincoln he had along a newspaperman named Kellogg. Reinstated, part of the expedition which his death was to project into history, the matter of Custer's personal ambition must be briefly examined in order to lend reason to the things he was now to do. A deceased authority said Custer told him at this time he intended to "cut loose from Terry this summer." It would be as difficult for you to prove he *didn't* say this as it would be for me to prove he *did* say it. Similarly, allegations that he had presidential aspirations are as poorly founded, but it is consistent with his character as we know it, that he believed himself, not only invincible, but superior to the great majority of mankind. He was truly a paradox; possessing a fine sense of humour, courage beyond measure, he was nonetheless capable of the most wanton brutalities in a day when such things were looked upon with much less horror than they are today. His spirit was bold and hardy; it was also impatient and imperious. He was among the strictest of disciplinarians although with no great record for aptitude in this field himself. That he was heartily disliked by those above him

47

was no secret. That he very likely felt a strong urge to show himself superior to them is plausible. That he fully intended to make his campaign against the Sioux and Northern Cheyennes a personal triumph is beyond question, and now, back as acting-commander of the 7th Cavalry, he was in a position to put into execution his private schemes. His second in command was Marcus A. Reno whose immediate subordinate was bulllike, taciturn Captain Frederick W. Benteen, whom Custer did not like, and who returned the animosity with equal cordiality.

But Captain Benteen was not the only man in the 7th with a personal dislike of Custer, or for Custer's relatives who went with the expedition. In fact the 7th was made up largely of recruits; it was not an old regiment; there was more than the usual distrust and animosity within its ranks, among officers and men. It was under this cloud that the 7th marched out of Fort Abraham Lincoln 17th May, 1876. Colonel Custer was attired in fringed buckskins. He was not wearing the red shirt which he customarily used on field service against Indians and by which he was known to them. Nor was his hair shoulder-length as heretofore. In fact Colonel Custer and "Lonesome Charley" Reynolds looked very much alike by the time General Terry's command reached the Powder River. They were about the same height and build, both had a drooping moustache, short hair, and buckskins.

At the Powder General Terry detached Major Reno with a small force to scout the countryside. Reno stretched his orders a little and made a wide sweep towards the fateful Rosebud where he located fresh Indian sign by the river. Reno followed this trail until satisfied which way the hostiles were going then returned and reported, saying he estimated the village to be one of "about three hundred lodges."

Terry's camp was beside the Yellowstone River where a supply boat, the *Far West*, lay at anchor. Terry called for a meeting of officers aboard the *Far West*. There, he laid before Colonels Custer and Gibbon his plan for proceeding against the hostiles. It was evident that somewhere not far distant was a large force of hostiles; it was not pressing that he know *exactly* where they were so long as he knew they were within a given locality, for it was his idea that Custer take the 7th Cavalry to the Rosebud River and travel up it until he found the trail Major Reno had reported. He was then to proceed very cautiously, keeping scouts out all around, until he found the hostile village or villages; he was then to bivouac, send General Terry word through scout George

Herendeen where the Indians were, and wait until the balance of the command was in position to attack.

The officers discussed General Terry's plan at some length. There was no doubt in any of their minds what was intended. The general asked Custer what kind of time he thought he could make and Custer replied thirty miles a day. Using this as a basis the three officers then plotted one another's routes so as to be more or less parallel, consequently within supporting distance should any of the columns be attacked, or if they were not, so that each would arrive before the hostiles at about the same time. Specifically, Terry did not want Custer to arrive in the Little Bighorn Valley before he and Colonel Gibbon were on hand to support him.

When the plan was agreed upon General Terry for some reason suggested to Custer that perhaps he should take Gibbon's command and go with Custer. Custer said he would prefer making the sortie alone and expressed the belief that the 7th would be strong enough to protect itself against any band of hostiles it might encounter. Terry acquiesced; in fact it was the prevailing belief that the hostiles were not strong. Just why Custer — and Terry — should have believed the 7th Cavalry regiment was capable of handling all the Indians it might encounter can possibly be attributed to the common notion that the Sioux and Cheyennes would flee at sight of soldiery. Otherwise there is no sound reason for their belief at all. It has been stated that Custer, Terry, Gibbon and Crook had no idea how strong the Indians were. This appears very unlikely; aside from the much-experienced Charley Reynolds, there were many other scouts and 'breeds, including Custer's own "Mitch" Bouyer (half-blood Crow who hated Colonel Custer and his brother Captain Tom, both, in private), not to mention George Herendeen, all of whom most certainly knew how strong the hostiles *could* be, and in fact did know, for they had accurately estimated the number of Indians on the warpath some time before. Major Reno's scouts had estimated the trail up the Rosebud at three hundred lodges. Others had reported greater numbers of hostiles even before Terry's command had left Fort Lincoln. In spite of this Terry said later: "I shared his (Custer's) confidence."

Perhaps Terry's assurance was based on the fact that he meant for Custer to take a battery of Gatling guns with him, but Custer declined saying the guns might "embarrass me," meaning evidently that they might slow him down, for after he left the camp on the Yellowstone he did not adhere to the agreed-upon thirty miles a day, but pushed his men and horses to the limit obviously in order to find the Indians before either Terry or Gibbon did. In ignoring this pivotal point of co-ordination Custer doomed General Terry's strategy, which was simply a smaller tactical employment of the over-all plan of campaign; the prevention of escape and a unified assault, designed to contain the hostiles while the column of Crook — thought to be pressing forward as earlier agreed upon — came up to reinforce Terry and aid in crushing the Indians. It was not known of course that Crook had been engaged on the Rosebud and was even then retreating.

Gibbon was to time his entrance into the Bighorn Valley so as to coincide with Custer's advance, and Terry was to support both advance detachments while sealing off the avenue of escape against the Indians. There were three factors which abrogated the chances of success: Crook was not coming up; Custer had ambitious plans of his own; the Indians were not trying to escape.

Before Custer left the Yellowstone General Terry sent him a note saying: ". . . It is, of course, impossible to give you any definite instructions in regard to this movement, and were it not impossible to do so, the Department Commander places too much confidence in your zeal, energy and ability to impose upon you precise orders which might hamper your action when nearly in contact with the enemy. He will, however, indicate to you his own views of what your action should be, and he desires that you should conform to them unless you shall see sufficient reason for departing from them. . . ."

Custer wrote his wife: "Mouth of Rosebud, June 21, 1876. . . . Look on my map and you will find our present location on the Yellowstone, about midway between Tongue River and the Big Horn. The scouting-party has returned. They saw the trail and deserted camp of a village. . . . The trail was about one week old. The scouts reported that they could have overtaken the village in one day and a half. I am now going to take up the trail where the scouting-party turned back. I fear their failure to follow up the Indians has imperilled our plans by giving the village an intimation of our presence. Think of the valuable time lost! But I feel hopeful of accomplishing great results. I will move directly up the valley of the Rosebud. . . . I like campaigning with pack-mules much better than with wagons, leaving out the question of luxuries. We take no tents and desire none.

"I now have some Crow scouts with me, as they are familiar with the country. They are magnificent-looking men, so much handsomer and more Indian-like than any we have ever seen, and so jolly and sportive; nothing of the gloomy, silent red-man about them. They have formally given themselves to me, after the usual talk. In their speech they said they had heard that I never abandoned a trail; that when my food gave out I ate mule. That was the kind of a man they wanted to fight under; they were willing to eat mule too.

"I am going to send six 'Ree scouts to Powder River with the mail; from there it will go with other scouts to Fort Buford. . . ."

The next morning, early, Custer wrote Elizabeth another letter: ". . . I have but a few moments to write, as we move at twelve, and I have my hands full of the preparations for the scout. . . . Do not be anxious about me. You would be surprised to know how closely I obey your instructions about keeping with the column. I hope to have a good report to send you by the next mail. . . . A success will start us all towards Lincoln. . . ."

He left Terry's base camp on the Yellowstone at noon, 22nd June, 1876. The 7th Cavalry was about six hundred strong. In addition to the soldiers he had about thirty-six Arikari and Crow scouts including his favourite 'Ree, Bloody Knife. Custer, and in fact the great majority of officers felt that his force was capable of fighting and defeating twelve hundred Indians, a ratio of two-to-one.

Chapter Two

CUSTER followed Reno's trail in a general way until he came to the river; there he turned southward. It required two days to accomplish this although he travelled more than thirty miles a day. Bivouacing the evening of the 24th he ordered scouts out to locate the far-ranging vedettes he had sent ahead of the column earlier in the day.

Meanwhile the hostiles whom we left on the east side of the Little Bighorn River had struck camp and gone straggling downriver because the spies who had been watching Crook's force reported much game in that direction. This particular area was noted as a great hunting ground; Indians had used it as a larder since earliest times; it was customary for them to hunt here in great numbers. Innumerable bands converged there every summer. They met, frequently combined villages and generally spent the warm months acquiring the stores needed for survival through the bitter winters.

The most feasible explanation of what ensued must take into consideration the lateness, the dusk, and ultimately the darkness. Custer's scouts had found no Indians and the hostiles seeking game found neither soldiers nor their allies although both were approaching one another. It is not impossible that they passed one another in the night at sufficient distance to preclude discovery. Regardless of *how* it happened, both parties were separated by the narrowing distance between two rivers.

By this time also, the hostile village had been increased greatly by an influx of "tame" Indians and other hunting bands, not to mention various groups of other sub-tribes of the Sioux and Northern Cheyenne confederacy. There were even some Southern Cheyennes, by no means as warlike as their cousins. Even a few Arapahoes and Blackfeet Sioux were along. Many of the warrior-societies had sent strongheart warriors in response to the news of Crook's defeat on the Rosebud. Ostensibly the hostiles were hunting, but as always the hunter had only to shift his feet to re-align his sights from a deer to a man. Indians from as far off as Canada were now with the hostiles. The acknowledged chieftain was The Bull Who Sits Among Us, sub-chieftains numbered about fifty; in total the hostiles numbered approximately forty-five hundred to five thousand warriors, excluding non-combatants. It has been said this was the greatest gathering of Northwestern

Indians to that time. Additionally, more arrived every day or so.

Before Custer arrived in the vicinity the Indians had crossed the Little Bighorn River westerly, gone streaming down the valley. As was customary the Northern Cheyennes were in the lead, Sitting Bull's Hunkpapas in the rear. After about ten miles had been covered the Indians halted and formed camp circles. Because the Hunkpapas came last they were obliged to take the farthest extremity for their camp. According to Siouxian precedent this was as it should be. The village was established close to Medicine Dance Creek (Reno Creek). One section of the trail to this camp had been what Marcus Reno had discovered in his scout inland from the Yellowstone; his report of some three hundred and fifty tipis covered only this one avenue of approach to the village. This trail was about a quarter of a mile wide, with very plain travois marks.

In veering inland the Indians had swung away from the oncoming 7th Cavalry under Custer. They did not know Custer was close by, nor did Custer know how close he was to his prey. If it appears ironic that Major Reno came so close to making a startling discovery — and despite Custer's reference to his wife of Reno's failure to press forward — Reno's specific orders from General Terry had been not to go beyond the spot where he located Indian sign. In fact Reno violated those orders in even following the trail as far as he did. But nevertheless he could not have determined how great the gathering of Indians was without making a general sweep of the country for the hostiles were travelling separately, in bands and individual villages; their approaches were miles apart although their destinations were the same and in time they converged. Now Custer made the same mistake, for he assumed the trail he was following was of the only village in the area.

In time "Mitch" Bouyer and others made a fairly accurate estimation of the number of hostiles but by that time Custer was convinced in his own mind that the village was nowhere nearly as large as they said and would not be convinced otherwise. Forty-five hundred *Ozuye We Tawatas* — Men Of War — had never been encountered in one body before; every sign on the trail indicated they would not be encountered now.

On the other hand the Indians did not know that Custer was just beyond the high bluffs where they had established their village. They still had spies watching Crook but it was thought he was the only soldier-commander in the country. This appears odd in view of the great number of Indians who were constantly riding out, hunting, herding their horses, yet it was possible for Custer's 7th Cavalry to get close, bypassing through one of those unique slots of blindness, and this is what happened. Still, the day before he got into the Little Bighorn a few warriors reported seeing a dustcloud. This unquestionably was made by Custer's command. Nothing was done about it; bands of new arrivals were riding into the hostile camp every few hours, presumably it was thought the dustcloud was raised by one of these. There is also some reason to believe that the Cheyennes had made a detour en route to the valley and that their travois and horse-herds made a dustcloud. The old-time Cheyennes said no; they remembered making no such detour; that in retrospect the dustcloud could only have belonged to Custer.

The three hundred lodges Custer followed were only a very small part of the hostile village. The number of Indians has been estimated as high as twenty thousand people and as low as twelve thousand. Principal chieftains offer an indication of the tribes and sub-tribes represented: The Bull Who Sits (or Waits) Among Us, commonly called Sitting Bull, of the Hunkpapas; Kicking Bear, Big Road, Crazy Horse, of the Oglalas; Lame Deer of the Minneconjous; Hump of the Sansarcs; Old Bear, Dirty

Moccasin and Crazy Head, principal leaders of the Cheyennes, with their lesser leaders Lame White Man, Plenty Bears, Two Moons, Wolf Medicine, Left-Hand-Shooter, A-Crow-Cuts-His-Nose, White Hawk, Tall White Man, and others.

The question of Indian armament is debatable — like most other points regarding the battle. Army protagonists insist the Indians had been trading and stealing the latest repeating rifles, carbines and pistols since shortly after the Civil War. There is evidence to support the statement that traders did a good business throughout the Indians' troubles. However, since selling guns to Indians was illegal this traffic had to be carried on more or less with discretion which precluded any mass arming of hostiles. Moreover, not many Indians had the means to trade for good guns, and the best rebuttal of all was the fact that dead soldiers were found to be full of arrows, not bulletholes, after Custer's attack on the Little Bighorn. The Indians themselves said they did not have many good guns when they fought Custer; that the older warriors preferred the silent and accurate bow; that old-time trade-guns — smoothbore muskets — were in evidence but very few good repeating arms were used in the fight until they could be taken from dead soldiers, scouts and friendlies. Verification can be found in reports of visitors to the battlefield before the corpses were interred. The "corpses resembled pincushions stuck full of arrows. . . ."

That evening when Custer's 7th stopped behind the hills they were still many miles from the hostile village. That same evening the Indians had their horse herds driven to new grazing grounds farther out, each tribe having its own herders and horse-guards. In aggregate the Indian horses numbered not less than fifteen thousand head. Essentially this great a body of animals had to be driven over great distances in order to secure adequate feed. That night, with their horses driven far out, and with Custer out of sight, the Indians recited their coups on the Rosebud against Crook and had another wild and prolonged celebration, including social dances. These dances usually lasted all night long; this one was no exception.

During his forced-march earlier Custer's orders had precluded loud talking, bugle calls or the discharge of firearms. Each company commander had been required to report in person; no orders were shouted or relayed in loud voice. The packtrain had been screened and protected by friendlies and one company of soldiers. Everything had been handled expertly, stealthily, even to the point of attempting to minimise the tell-tale dustcloud — which had not been successful but which *had* been ignored by the Indians. In fact the 7th Cavalry, with a roster of forty per cent raw recruits, behaved perfectly on the trail. Later, after the disaster and the subsequent Court of Inquiry, Sergeant Culbertson of A Company testified: "Most of G Company were recruits; about half; and about a third of A Company. . . . The men had had very little training; they were very poor marksmen and would fire at random. They were brave enough but had not had the time nor opportunity to make soldiers. . . ."

A typical company of the 7th was forty-five men. Seven were detailed to the packtrain. One man was detached as flag-bearer. Another as hospital steward or medical-aid man. Another as orderly to the surgeon. In action the company could rely upon about thirty-five effectives, ten of whom would be detached as horse-holders; these might or might not participate in an action; generally they did not.

When his scouts returned and informed Custer the Indian trail he was following crossed over into the Bighorn Valley he called up his officers and said the march would be undertaken at once in order to place the command close to where it was supposed the hostiles were, by dawn. He proposed then to rest all day the 25th of

June and attack upon the 26th if the Indians had not moved. Of course this forced-march, aside from being needlessly hard on men and animals, put him more than a day in advance of Terry and Gibbon. It becomes obvious he had no intention of awaiting support nor of informing the other commanders of his fortune in locating hostiles, for he did not detach George Herendeen as ordered and send him to Terry with news.

Because of the total darkness and an unfamiliarity with the ground the command made very poor time. Custer called a halt two hours after midnight. He sent scouts out under Lieutenant Varnum to reconnoitre the country ahead. It was unexpectedly cold, contrasting with the hot, cloudless days of June. Varnum made for a pinnacle they had all noticed before nightfall, called the Crow's Nest. He arrived there sometime before dawn, was obliged to await daylight in order to see. Before sunup, at false-dawn, Varnum got a good view of the jumbled country below. The Crow scouts under "Mitch" Bouyer immediately drew Varnum's attention to what they said was a very large Indian village in the distance. They had first seen the huge horse-herd. They estimated the village as being thirteen miles away. Lieutenant Varnum could not make out the village but sent word back to Custer that it had been sighted. Crow's Nest, the promontory where Varnum waited, was high on the Wolf Mountain divide. The Wolf Mountains — or Little Chetish Mountains — lay between the valleys of the Rosebud and the Little Bighorn Rivers of southeast Montana. They were not actually a mountain range but rather a series of erosion-cut eminences dividing innumerable gullies and arroyos. Not far away the Little Bighorn River wound its crooked way northwesterly across the great prairies to the Bighorn River, approximately forty miles away. The Little Bighorn was a wide river with a clean, pebbled bottom; in places it was no more than two feet deep, but at other spots it exceeded five feet in depth. There were fords but in general the bank was soft and crumbly. The valley itself was rolling, richly carpeted with tall, sweet grass. Groves of cottonwoods and box elders dotted its great width and depth. Where Varnum stood, waiting at the Crow's Nest, was considerable evidence that the promontory had been used for many hundreds of years as a tribal watchtower. Near him stood Hairy Moccasin who had first sighted the smoke from many Sioux cooking-fires. Then Goes Ahead was the Crow who had sighted the horse-herd. The Crow, White Man Runs Him told Varnum there were more Sioux and Cheyennes down in the village than Son-Of-The-Morning-Star's — Custer's

65

name among the Crows — soldiers had bullets. Varnum's Arikari companions, satisfied after a personal study of their own, broke into trilling war songs. Varnum and the Crows told them to be quiet. Charley Reynolds, who up to now had said nothing — the Indians called him Lucky Man — now set his field-glasses to his eyes and verified with a nod to Varnum that it was a large village.

When word arrived back at the bivouac ten miles away that the hostiles had been sighted Colonel Custer ordered an immediate advance. With several companions Custer rode on ahead to the Crow's Nest. He was met by Reynolds who led him to the place of vantage but all he could see was the bluffs which partially hid the hostile encampment; he told Reynolds he was imagining things, that there was no sign of a hostile camp that he could see. "Lonesome Charley" then handed Custer his field-glasses and after some additional study Custer said: "It's possible. You may be right. . . ." He then returned to the column after some additional conversation during which he was told by one of the Crows that some Sioux warriors had seen the men on the promontory, and called another meeting of his officers. He told them that he had seen no village but that others swore they had and therefore he thought it likely the hostiles were not far off. The command was then dismounted, for Custer did not intend to attack that day. Men and animals were tired. He planned to make another forced-march that night and attack the village on the 26th, as previously explained.

The officers were making coffee and talking when a noncommissioned officer reported that one of the packs had come loose some time in the night and had fallen off a mule. He was directed to take a small detachment and back-track until he found it. It was thought the pack contained ammunition. After an hour or so of riding the sergeant topped out over a slight land-swell and saw not only his pack but a small party of Indians examining it. One Indian boy (Deeds, a nephew of Sitting Bull) was sitting on the box, his companions were riding their horses back and forth across the fresh trail of six hundred shod horses, studying the ground, or standing close to the pack talking. One of the Cheyennes saw the soldiers on the hill and cried out a warning whereupon the dismounted Indians leapt upon their horses and fled with their companions — not towards the valley but southeastward. The soldiers fired several rounds, retrieved the pack — which contained hardtack not bullets — and rode back to the command where it was reported to Custer that there were Indians behind the column. (The Indians have a version of this episode: They say that the white sergeant [Curtis of F Company] shot and killed Deeds who was eating hardtack from the pack; that the other bucks fled *into* Bighorn Valley and spread the alarm.)

About this time the "wolves" at the Crow's Nest saw a body of Sioux warriors racing across the valley below. While they watched one of these riders reined up his mount and rode it in a tight little circle, indicating that the enemy had been sighted. Interpreting this to mean themselves, the Crows sent word to Custer. Actually what the hostiles had probably seen was the dustcloud made by the command coming up, led by Custer. Additionally, however, some hostile hunters were seen sitting their horses well beyond rifle-range, watching the scouts on Crow's Nest. Beyond a question of a doubt the invaders had been seen and perhaps identified; at any rate enough encounters had been made to preclude additional need for secrecy or stealth, and in fact unless an immediate advance was made the hostiles would be fully alerted by the 26th, when Custer intended attacking them. Among the Crows, 'Rees and white scouts at the Crow's Nest there was a sense of forboding. When Custer came up "Mitch" Bouyer told him of the excited warriors who had sighted them then raced away towards the village.

Bouyer, half-French, half-Sioux, married to a Crow, urged Custer not to wait until the next day to attack. Custer answered him shortly and he retired where the other Crows were sitting in silence. George Herendeen came up and told Custer that he had found ample evidence that a Sioux war-party was scouting behind the column; that it was his opinion that the hostiles had them under surveillance and knew everything they were doing. Custer sent his brother Tom back to the waiting column with an order for all officers to assemble, and all troopers to prepare for an inspection of their arms. He had changed his plans, as Bouyer had urged, and was obviously going to attack on the 25th. As soon as this was interpreted to the Indian allies they began making preparations for combat. The Arikaris, generally smaller, darker, than the Crows, stripped down to g-strings and mocasins, opened their medicine bundles and began adorning their bodies with sacred and protective symbols, as did the Crows.

Custer left the point, returned to the command which had already held weapons' inspection. The rumour that he would lead an attack today was lent substance when a bugler was directed to sound Officers' Call. Obviously he no longer expected to take the hostiles by surprise; the bugle-call carried for miles in that clear, sparkling air. His council of officers was brief. When it was over each officer returned to his command and ordered the men to mount, form in columns of two. The trail they were using — called by the hostiles Lodgepole Trail — was narrow. Not far from where Colonel Custer sat his horse the grey and ageing newspaperman Mark Kellogg — whom the Indians also knew and had named Man-Who-Makes-Paper-Talk — was astride the stubby-legged little grey mule he rode, and which occasioned mirth among friendlies and soldiers alike. Kellogg was a contrast to Custer. He wore no arms and carried a black satchel slung over one shoulder in which he carried the media of his trade. He was colourless and quiet.

As the troops moved past, Custer hailed White Man Runs Him and directed that he go ahead of the column and scout the countryside. Behind the scout Custer rode with Kellogg, behind them came the long line of soldiers. When they had reached a summit and started down the valley side Custer called a halt and hailed Adjutant of the 7th Cavalry, Lieutenant William A. Cooke, who possessed the finest set of whiskers in the regiment; in fact the finest set at Fort Lincoln. Here Custer made the fatal division of his command. Cooke transcribed the orders on to paper: Captain

Frederick W. Benteen was to lead his "battalion" of three companies southwesterly and prevent the escape of the hostiles in that direction. Benteen took no Indian scouts with him. Major Reno and his "battalion" of three companies was directed to cross the meandering creek which bears his name and strike for the village. Captain Thomas M. McDougall with one company was to act as escort for the packtrain and Colonel Custer, with five companies, intended to remain on the right bank of Reno Creek parallel to Reno in the advance. It was then a few minutes past high noon. The Indian scouts were far ahead; they knew that valley very well for when there were no Sioux or Cheyennes around they hunted it too.

The advance was resumed. Within a few minutes Captain Benteen's detachment was lost to sight in the broken country to the southwest. The friendlies far ahead halted and waited until the division of Custer's command had been completed, the advance begun again. It was Sunday, 25th June, 1876. The weather was perfect; the sky an immaculate, pale blue. It was warm without being excessively hot. There was a stillness to the air. Quite a few miles off the Indians were generally unalarmed; the reason for this involves some explaining.

On the west bank of the Little Bighorn

River there was a flat plateau which stood somewhat higher than the surrounding country. It was an ideal place for a camp. Beyond it, across the river, the land rose gradually to a height of about two hundred feet and there was another plateau. From the first slight level place the Indian encampment stretched north and south almost five miles. There were seven large tipi villages, none of them under a quarter mile diameter. Beyond each circle were horses and industrious squaws working over meat-drying racks or pegged-out, freshly scraped hides. There was considerable human traffic, quite a little dust and smoke from hundreds of cooking fires. The custom which had guided Indian villages travelling in consort since earliest times dictated where each band camped, and within each camp-circle each Indian family had its own place; it was never difficult to locate a family although hundreds of hide tipis appeared at first glance to be identical with one another. Tipi decorations denoted the coups of each warrior who resided therein; his great hunts, his outstanding feats of statesmanship.

The Northern Cheyennes were established at the extreme northerly end of the village. Included among their tipis were the residences of some Gros Ventres and five Arapahoes. Altogether they numbered close to two thousand people. Away from the river and somewhat westerly of the Cheyennes was the Oglala Sioux camp-circle, who in some respects were closer to the Cheyennes than to other sub-tribes of their own nation. Camped along the river itself were the lodges of the Brûlé or Burnt Thigh Sioux. Next to them were the Sansarc Sioux, allied to the Burnt Thighs by reason of an over-all designation which grouped seven Sioux sub-tribes under the heading of Teton-Sioux. Camped with the Sansarcs was a strong band of Two Kettle Sioux — also called Teton-Sioux.

On the other side of the river were the very powerful and warlike Minneconjou Sioux. Also on the south side of the river, but some distance inland, was the camp of the combined Blackfeet Sioux, some Assiniboins, the Santee Sioux, Yanktonnai, and Yankton Sioux.

At the farthest southern end of the great encampment was the village of about three thousand Hunkpapa Sioux — Sitting Bull's village. It was here that a great coming and going went on, for although there were innumerable renowned warriors at this last great encampment of the free Indians, Sitting Bull was generally acknowledged as the greatest medicine man present.

Old Red Cloud was not present; his eighteen-year-old son Jack Red Cloud was, but he had shamed himself by running at the Battle of the Rosebud — Crook's Crows had taken his warbonnet and his carbine and laughed in his face; had scorned killing him, striking him with their horse-quirts instead. His father had refused to take up the hatchet saying if the white people broke their word it was a bad thing, but nothing, not even war against his people, could make him break his word. But Red Cloud was an old man in 1876; he had many scars, many old wounds on his wasted body; it was difficult for him to move and he was nearly blind. His Oglalas were under the leadership of Big Road and He-Dog. Also among the Oglala warriors was a man named Crazy Horse.

Significantly at this time on the Red Cloud Reservation every buck-Indian of warrior age was gone. When this information was reluctantly relayed to the Army by the Indian Bureau it had been transmitted to Phil Sheridan in Chicago who hastened to send a warning to General Terry — too late. But the Indians had not gathered together for war; they would fight given an opportunity any time, but in June, 1876, they were in the Bighorn Valley to hunt, process food for winter, and hold several ritual observances. They had held one — the Sun Dance which was held every late spring — on the Rosebud ten days earlier. There Sitting Bull had given one hundred pieces of skin from his arms to The Great Mystery, *Wakan Tanka* — The Great Spirit. It had been during this rite while sitting motionless staring at the sun all day long that he had had the vision showing American soldiers and their Indian allies falling head first into the Indian encampment, dead, which had been interpreted to mean a great Indian triumph. Crook's defeat on the Rosebud followed, but Sitting Bull and others said that was not the battle the dream indicated. It was in these numbers and in this state of mind that the Indians now heard of the coming of white soldiers and enemy Indians. But, because the camps were so distant from one another the time required to warn them of Custer's advance was greater than was allowed and the majority of the hostiles did not know they were being attacked for a long time after battle was joined.

Reno, riding down the valley across the creek from Custer, had Captains French and Myles Moylan, and Lieutenant McIntosh, in command of A, M, and G, companies. Benteen who was by this time too far away to offer support or take an active part in the battle soon to develop, had H, D, and K, companies, while the force under Custer was officered by his brother Captain Tom Custer, his brother-in-law Lieutenant Calhoun, and Captains Keogh and Yates. Colonel Custer's other younger brother was also along but because he was too young for service he rode with the civilian packers. This was Boston Custer familiarly called "Boss." Custer's nephew "Autie" Reed who was also a youth, accompanied his uncle's column too.

Benteen's orders were, first, to take his one hundred and twenty-five men and determine if any Indians were camped to the left of the advancing column, and if they were to return to the command. His second orders, sent while he was carrying out the first orders, were to attack any hostiles he found. While Benteen was seeking Indians another order came directing him to go over into the next valley if he found no Indians closer, then, if he failed to find Indians in the second valley to go on over into the third valley. Benteen was angered but he persevered. The country was particularly uneven and mountainous; the trip was unrewarding; the travel was hard on men and horses. Those were the last orders Frederick Benteen ever received from Colonel George Custer. "When I received my orders from Custer," Benteen said later, "to separate myself from the command, I had no instructions to unite with Reno or anyone else. There was no plan at all. . . . In General Custer's mind there was a belief that there were no Indians and no villages. . . . I was (sent) to pitch into them and let him know. And if I had found them, the distance would have been so great that we would have been wiped out before he could get to us."

Major Reno said: "There was no plan communicated to us; if one existed the subordinate commanders did not know it. . . ."

Sergeant Culbertson said: "I heard Captain Weir ask Captain Moylan if, when he was Adjutant, General Custer ever gave him any particular orders about doing anything. Captain Moylan said 'no,' that when he was Adjutant, General Custer never told him what he was going to do. . . ."

Under these circumstances Colonel Custer led about two hundred and twenty-five men into the Bighorn Valley along the right, or east, side of Reno Creek. Paralleling him southward was Reno with about one hundred and thirty-five men. By this time there could no longer be any doubt that a large village was close by. There were the barefoot tracks of many horses; there were also moccasin tracks ahead and behind the columns. In this fashion, with Reno Creek between them, the paralleling forces advanced about seven miles. The terrain was such that it was frequently necessary for one party or the other to skirt hillocks and gullies but they were never more than a half mile apart.

Early in the afternoon Colonel Custer rode up on to a small eminence and waved his hat at Reno who interpreted the signal to mean he was to cross the creek and join forces with Custer. This was done and the combined force continued to advance slowly until it came upon a lone tipi set back a short distance from the creek. Around this lodge were signs of freshly struck tipis. The scouts ranging ahead had found this solitary lodge some time before. Shortly before the scouts had arrived upon the scene some Sioux warriors had dashed up and warned mourning kinsmen of the dead man inside the tipi that enemies were approaching, for them to make haste in the direction of the main encampment while the warriors stood off the foe. No defence was attempted however for shortly after the arrival of Custer's scouts the main column came into sight and the warriors prudently withdrew; sat their horses in the distance and watched.

Inside the lodge was a dead warrior. This tipi was located about three miles from the confluence of Reno Creek and the Little Bighorn River. The dead man was Old She Bear a Sansarc, brother of Chief Circling Bear. He had been shot through the bowels and both hips in the fight on the Rosebud; it had taken him several days to die. He had been particularly conspicuous under

Crazy Horse in the fight against Crook. After he had died the village had moved about four miles away and only his widow and a few close kinsmen had remained. While Old She Bear still lived, in fact when it seemed to his tribesmen that he was rallying, they resorted to an ancient rite to determine whether he was going to recover or not. A badger was hunted and killed, its entrails removed, the blood caught and allowed to congeal. Old She Bear was then raised up to look into the dried blood; if the reflection there showed a young man's features he would live, if the features of an old man he would die. Old She Bear is said to have seen an old man's face; at any rate he died and when Custer's friendlies found his body laid out on the burial platform within the lodge — the face painted completely red — they set fire to the tipi.

Scout Girard rode ahead a short distance and mounted a slight hill. Down country a ways he saw a band of about half a hundred warriors streaking it for the main village. Although the Indians were riding away they did not act particularly excited or afraid. Girard turned and called down to Colonel Custer: "Here are your Indians, running like hell."

Custer promptly ordered the Crow scouts to pursue the fleeing hostiles. The Crows made no move to obey and Custer castigated them threatening to disarm them and take their horses. He additionally ordered them to move back so his soldiers could pass them. The reason for the Crow refusal seems to devolve upon "Mitch" Bouyer whose ride ahead convinced him more than ever that the number of their enemies was overpowering. He had evidently passed this along to the other Crows, who were now depressed and reluctant to advance further into the valley. It is claimed that after his last sortie Bouyer told the Crows to leave, to go anywhere, but not to go with Custer down into the valley for there were too many enemies down there.

Custer then had Adjutant Cooke carry the order to Major Reno to pursue the Indians with his command: "General Custer directs that you take as fast a gait as you deem prudent," the order read, "and charge afterward, and you will be supported by the whole outfit." There is disagreement among authorities on the exact context of this message but not on its purport; none disagree with the final words: ". . . you will be supported by the whole outfit."

By this time there was no doubt but that a very large village lay ahead. Every subsequent account mentions the great pall of dust which hung over the distant encampment, although at this time no one had yet *seen* the village with the possible — but not probable — exception of "Mitch" Bouyer and perhaps one or two of the other Indian scouts. It was said the dustcloud was caused by a herd of buffalo; this was quickly rebutted with the observation that the cloud was not moving. Custer again said he did not believe there was any exceptionally large village ahead. In fact, his excitement over the band of Dog Soldiers Girard had seen indicated that he thought these were all the warriors close by.

Benteen meanwhile was still climbing from one valley to another, riding farther and farther away from the main column.

Marcus Reno led his "battalion" out in a chopping trot, Scouts Girard, Charley Reynolds, George Herendeen and the Arikaris accompanied the column. Custer's favourite 'Ree Bloody Knife was also along as was Isaiah Dorman, the only Negro with the command. Dorman — what the Indians called a "black white man" — had lived with the Sioux and spoke their language well. (Indians did not scalp Negroes believing they had no souls which would be doomed to darkness through scalping.)

Several of the friendlies were compelled to drop back as Reno's force swept forward due to weak and tiring mounts. These ultimately joined the packtrain escort under McDougall. Bouyer's Crows did not advance with Reno. One of them, seeing a dustcloud, said the Sioux were fleeing. To ascertain whether this was true or not Custer ordered the Crows White Swan and Half Yellow Face to ride up a nearby ridge and see, but they did not understand Custer's *wibluto* — sign-talk — and thought he was sending them after Reno. They both whipped up their horses and went racing after the distant command. Bouyer then led other Crows up the hill while Custer began an advance with his five companies along Reno's route. By this time Reno was no longer visible. Bouyer reported the Indians in flight. This mistake can reasonably be adduced to Reno's dustcloud for the hostiles still were in general ignorant of the fact that they were under attack; had made no move to strike their camp. There was some scattered excitement at the village but it had not spread much at this time.

So far as Colonel George Custer's unified command is concerned known facts end here. He had said he would support Reno and in fact he initially moved as though to do so, but somewhere en route to the site of the village and subsequent battle he veered off. Possibly in order to strike the hostiles from another quarter, which is the prevalent belief, or perhaps so as to arrive before the village when the Indians were concentrating upon Reno, drive up through or cut across to confuse or overwhelm reinforcements hastening up where Reno was battling. No one will ever know what Custer intended; all that can be substantiated is that he told Reno he would support him, and he did not.

Lieutenant Cooke and Captain Myles Keogh rode with Reno as far as the river crossing. There they both turned back and joined Custer's five companies.

Most of the Indian allies had accompanied Reno's column. When they saw the horde of Sioux and Cheyennes streaming up the valley to meet them they were aghast. Several of the white scouts turned back to carry the news to Custer of the hostiles' numbers.

Cooke and Keogh were encountered and told of the overwhelming force arrayed against Reno. The hostiles were not fleeing as expected but seemed intent upon pitched battle. Cooke said he would carry the information to Custer. With that the link between the commands was broken for ever.

Reno crossed the Little Bighorn River about two-thirty in the afternoon. Custer was about a mile behind when Reno formed his "battalion" in the timber across from the mouth of Ash Creek. Ordered it to dismount, then re-mount after checking horses, saddles and arms. He sent a courier to Custer telling him that he had hostiles in unexpected numbers in his front. He then led his command at a brisk trot towards the oncoming hostiles. Lieutenant Varnum was ahead with the scouts. When the dust cleared sufficiently for him to appraise the oncoming enemy he dropped back upon Reno's main column, fanned out a little and swept along with the command which Reno led to within a quarter of a mile of the village at a gallop, in company-front.

The Indians meanwhile had halted their advance. They were arrayed in a great line across the trail leading into the village. As Reno swept closer the hostiles charged forward then fell back as though attempting to bait the soldiers into the village proper. It was here that Charley Reynolds said: "Someone had better tell Long Hair the Indians aren't running."

But this was only one of the seven villages. In another a small Cheyenne boy out gathering grasshoppers for fish-bait heard running horses and climbed a bank to see who was passing. The Indian riders were unfamiliar. He ran down to his village crying out. Several Cheyenne men ran out to see and recognised the Arikaris. Before they overcame their astonishment they saw a blue line of soldiers approaching in a charge. They fled howling an alarm.

The Arikaris were on Reno's left. Their instructions had been to hit the hostiles' horse-herds, scatter or capture them. It had been their charge on this mission that had been discovered by the Cheyennes. Bloody Knife and 'Ree managed to capture three Sioux horses. He drove these back where the faint-hearts were and turned them over to other scouts, then hurried to catch up with Reno's troopers. The first warning many of the Indians had that a battle was imminent was when they heard gunfire and later saw the passage of bullets through their lodges. By this time the owners of the foremost tipis in Reno's path were howling and fleeing in every direction, adding to an already deafening tumult — nothing unusual in an Indian encampment the size of this one.

Reno's first volley cut through the tipis. Women ran out screaming, grabbed their children in the bedlam and fled. Warriors grabbed their weapons and ran out where horses were. This pandemonium, added to the blinding dust, undoubtedly saved many an Indian from death as the soldiers charged the village.

Reno was stopped in a narrow part of the valley, roughly in line of fire of the Hunkpapa lodges, last in the line of camp-circles, and also one of the most numerous and warlike of the villages. The fight had been in progress some time before the adjoining camps were alerted; it was in fact late in the afternoon before the Cheyennes heard that the Hunkpapas were under attack, then the Cheyenne old men ran through their village crying the alarm. Some Sioux who had brought the news added to the din with their cries, begging the Cheyenne warriors to ride hastily the intervening four miles and aid their allies. A Cheyenne witness to the consternation and excitement said: "The air was so full of dust I could not see where to go." He nevertheless mounted his horse and started towards the scene of battle. "I kept my horse headed in the direction of movement by the crowd of Indians on horseback," he added, and: "I was led out and around and far beyond the Uncpapa campcircle. Many hundreds of Indians on horseback were dashing to and fro in front of a body of soldiers. The soldiers were on level valley ground and were shooting with rifles. Not many bullets were being sent back at them, but thousands of arrows were falling among them. . . ."

It was here in the face of stiff Sioux and Cheyenne resistance that Lieutenant Varnum began to have trouble holding the Crows and Arikaris together. The Crows appeared to have no stomach for the fight; the 'Rees fought desperately and defensively. The Crow reluctance eventually permeated the entire force of friendlies with

Reno's command and most of them finally broke and fled. A Crow named Curly, who later claimed to be the only survivor of the battle, was said to be among Reno's little band of friendlies before the village. After he deserted Reno's command he is said to have withdrawn to a distant hillside from where he witnessed the entire battle and later is said to have shot down and killed an escaping Army officer, presumably from Custer's command. This officer was shot through the body; to this day the location of his grave is unknown to the War Department. Only two men alive today know its location. Had the Crow scout Curly permitted this man to escape there would have been one survivor from Custer's column.

By the time Major Reno's command was near the village its horses were excited and barely manageable. The din of battle did nothing to alleviate this condition. One soldier's horse bolted carrying him straight into the mass of Indians. In a freakish and momentary break in the dustcloud Reno saw, directly in front of him, thousands of excited Indians. At that moment a volley of gunfire on his left threw the friendlies into confusion and they fled rearward. Only a handful remained with the soldiers; among these was Bloody Knife.

Reno raised his arm to halt the column. In his rear was a small but dense wood.

The valley was rather narrow here. Coming out of a gully to his left were the hostiles who had fired upon the friendlies. Here two more soldiers, riding horses maddened with fright or wounds and out of control, carried their riders into the ranks of Indians.

The Indians were shouting "Brave up!" to one another; the age-old cry among the Sioux: "It is a good day to die!" could be distinguished over the bedlam of gunfire and the screams of injured horses. The Indians facing Reno were constantly being reinforced by warriors from other camps. Gall, war-leader of the Hunkpapas, rallied his men in a bull-bass. The soldiers were shooting high. Where one small band of Indians stood leaves fell from the trees where gunfire swept overhead. An Indian named Iron Hawk tried to mount his horse but the animal kept jerking away, panicky from the noise and excitement. Not far off another warrior leapt upon his horse and raced towards the sound of battle, forgetting to take his weapons. Still another, Black Elk by name, rode to combat with two six-guns; he watched the soldiers shoot and was surprised to see that many were actually firing their guns into the air, pulling triggers before lowering the pieces to their shoulders for aiming.

In the Oglala camp there was rumour of an attack down by the Hunkpapa village.

Crazy Horse only half believed this; even the noise in the distance, the dust and clamour did not necessarily mean much for Indian camps were always full of both. But he made preparations for battle: First he made protective hail-spots on his body with spittle-mixed yellow ochre, then he sprinkled ground gopher-dust over himself and his horse — this would deceive the soldiers as well as their bullets. The rumours grew and persisted. Crazy Horse left his lodge when the rituals had been completed and called upon the Oglala fighting men. He said: "Hiyupa!" and they went with him after their horses.

By this time Reno's position was in great peril. The men fought well and desperately. If there was time to think they must have wished fervently for Custer's arrival. Bloody Knife and Young Hawk stood fast. Another 'Ree, Bob Tailed Bull was caught by the Sioux horsemen, surrounded and shot to death. Major Reno was fearful for his left where the press of hostiles under Black Moon was greatest. There was no way to withdraw and he could not force an advance. There had to be movement or quick support; his command was a motionless target and except for the dust the withering hostile marksmanship would have obliterated it, but in any case he could not stay where he was very long unless Custer came up. He was appalled at the numbers opposing him. These were already far in excess of what it had been thought the hostiles had in the valley, and occasionally when the dust permitted, he could see additional hordes hastening up from half a dozen different directions.

When he thought it no longer efficient to fight a-horseback Major Reno ordered his men to dismount. Every fourth trooper was detailed as horse-holder. The Sioux later said this was not a good thing to do for so long as a soldier was mounted on the big, strong cavalry horses, he might have at least made a run for safety; dismounted he had very little chance.

Reno tried to advance into the stand of woods which lay along the river and so well and unflinchingly did his men obey that they pushed forward steadily. By this time however Black Moon's pressure on the left had become a flanking movement; there was danger the hostiles might get into the trees first. If they did they could stampede Reno's horses. He was surrounded; although he feared this would happen he did not then know it already had been accomplished. The majority of his opponents were Sioux under Kicking Bear and Crazy Horse. According to witnesses Crazy Horse tried to get close enough to kill soldiers with his war-club. Firing in volleys the soldiers forced their enemy to give ground, but with greater mobility — they were still fighting from horseback — the Indians completed their surround and tightened it. The soldiers could progress no further. It probably was just as well for had they been able to reach and invest the nearest village their plight would have been infinitely worse than it eventually was in among the trees.

Major Reno told Lieutenant Wallace of G Company to send a scout to Custer with a plea for reinforcements, fast. Wallace approached 'breed Billy Jackson who was firing with a hand-gun at a charging Sioux warrior. Jackson did not reply in words when Wallace ordered him to try and reach Custer; he made the Indian sign for refusal and continued trying to shoot the Sioux. After a moment he turned and said: "I couldn't get through alive."

Reno was now about three hundred yards from the village. He was out-numbered approximately fifteen-to-one. If the accuracy of his men was less than average, Indian marksmanship was perhaps even worse; aside from inherent inaccuracy with fire-arms, being astride excited horses made their gunfire and arrow-fire considerably less lethal than they hoped for.

As additional warriors came up the Indian surround was strengthened still more. Seeing his peril, should the Indians cut him off from the trees and capture his horses,

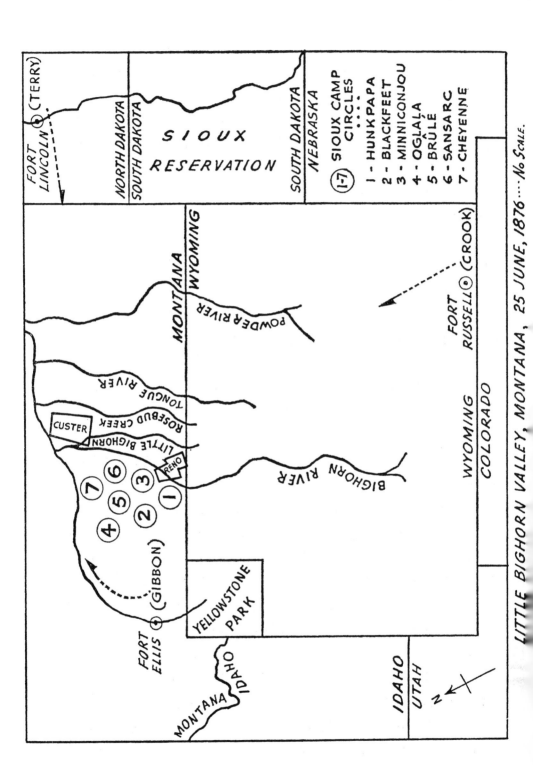

LITTLE BIGHORN VALLEY, MONTANA, 25 JUNE, 1876·····No Scale.

FORT LINCOLN ⊙ (TERRY)

NORTH DAKOTA
SOUTH DAKOTA

SIOUX
RESERVATION

SOUTH DAKOTA
NEBRASKA

⟨1-7⟩ SIOUX CAMP
CIRCLES

1 - HUNKPAPA
2 - BLACKFEET
3 - MINNICONJOU
4 - OGLALA
5 - BRÛLÉ
6 - SANSARC
7 - CHEYENNE

MONTANA
WYOMING

POWDER RIVER

FORT
RUSSELL ⊙ (CROOK)

WYOMING
COLORADO

TONGUE RIVER

ROSEBUD CREEK

CUSTER

LITTLE BIGHORN

RENO

BIGHORN RIVER

7 6
4 5 3
   2 1

FORT
ELLIS ⊙ (GIBBON)

YELLOWSTONE
PARK

MONTANA
IDAHO

IDAHO
UTAH

N

he ordered the detachment to change front so that the river was behind, the south end of the village on his right. In executing this manoeuvre the troops were able to prevent the flanking hostiles from getting between them and the trees, but they were not able to prevent Indians from infiltrating in small numbers where the horses were, all the while pouring a terrible fire into the exposed soldiery. Lieutenant Wallace said: ". . . I for the first time saw the village and the Indians were thick on our front and were pressing to our left and rear. After a short time it was reported that they were coming to the opposite bank (of the river) and were trying to get our horses. Company G was taken off the line and put back into the timber. The skirmish line soon had to fall back into the timber on account of the exhaustion of ammunition and Indians on our left and rear. After being there some time the Indians commenced firing from across the stream (river) fifty yards from us and in our rear in the timber. There was no protection where we were, and the other side of the bank. Word was passed that we would have to charge them as we were being surrounded. . . ."

Another officer, Lieutenant de Rudio, said: ". . . I started with five or six men to see (how far the Indians had penetrated the woods). I saw some Indians through the woods, downstream. . . . I noticed the company guidon on the bank . . . about forty feet away. I crawled up and grabbed it. There were twenty or thirty Indians about forty feet away. They fired a volley at me. . . . There were about two hundred Indians on our right when we were in the timber. . . ."

Sergeant Heyn was shot through the chest. He miraculously survived not only his wound but the battle, a feat not common on 25th June, 1876. Heyn's comrades bore him along in their retreat into the timber. Dead soldiers were left in the dust and grass beyond, where the fighting had started.

Four miles or more away an Arapaho named Sage was watering horses with Northern Cheyenne Two Moon not far from their village. They had seen, commented upon the great dustcloud far off where the Hunkpapa village was. A Sioux fighting-man came riding from the south making gestures and yelling that the encampment was under attack by white soldiers. Two Moon and Sage rode through the Cheyenne village crying for the warriors to get their weapons and horses. Excitement spread. Some of the squaws immediately began striking their lodges. Children ran after the horse-herds, bedlam ensued. Many of the old people stood around in bewilderment while files of warriors streamed through the village at the gallop brandishing their guns, bows, and singing their strong-heart and death chants. The painted, sweating Sioux buck yelled at the women to get out of the way; there was going to be a big fight; take care of the children. Most of the Cheyennes did not understand his dialect but few misunderstood his gestures. He soon led off southward with the Cheyennes hooting and racing behind him. There were not many men left to defend the Cheyenne circle.

By this time Reno's plight was grave. The hostiles sent men to creep through the undergrowth into the timber and set the grass afire. Among the Indians, Sitting Bull was puzzled; why had so small a force of soldiers attacked so large an Indian encampment; why had they charged the village, then dismounted and fallen back into the trees? White officers were not ordinarily fools. He began to warn the other leaders it must be some kind of a trap — the sending of such a small band against them; there had to be more to it. But the others, excited beyond reasoning, did not pay any attention, and about this time the deafening racket was increased when Black Moon and One Bull led a charge into the timber. Close to One Bull, Good Bear Boy was shot through the hips, fell from his horse bleeding heavily.

Then chief of camp-police Black Moon was killed. Good Bear Boy undertook to crawl back to the Indian lines before he was drained of blood.

One of Reno's troopers now broke away and began to run through the woods. The major called for him to stop, when he did not Reno shouted at Bloody Knife who was standing next to him to have the man stopped. Bloody Knife relayed the message to the Crow, White Swan, who immediately ran after the soldier, overtook him and in the ensuing encounter stabbed him to death. White Swan then went back to his place in the firing line. About this time, with Reno despairing of Custer's arrival and about to be compelled to make the decision which later brought court martial, Lieutenant de Rudio saw soldiers on the high bluffs across the river. Although the distance was considerable he said afterwards he recognised Custer's buckskin dress. (At least half a dozen others had similar clothing.) More plausible was his statement that he recognised Lieutenant Cooke's fabulous whiskers. Lieutenant Varnum also said he had seen the grey-horse company on the bluffs, but that it was not hastening to Reno's support; instead it was heading in the opposite direction. Of the two accounts Varnum's would appear most creditable. At that time Varnum did not know the grey-horse detachment was with Custer.

But Reno did not see the men on the bluffs across the river, and in any case could no longer hope for succour. His reserves were in the line, his ammunition running out, the foe increasing in numbers and ferocity. The decision he made was not as averse as has been implied; it was the manner in which he executed it which was faulty. By this time his men were borrowing ammunition from one another and many of their guns were jammed with expanded cartridge cases. Back in the timber was a small clearing formerly used by Indian vision-seekers. Reno passed the command for his men to rally on him there. Fortunately not many of his horses had been incapacitated and when the soldiers fell back they found most of their mounts already in the clearing. This manoeuvre of course permitted the Indians to press forward into the trees unopposed, which they did in great numbers. Finding the soldiers beyond in the clearing they howled in triumph and stepped up the volume of their fire. Reno's hat was shot off. He tied his handkerchief around his head to keep his hair from his eyes. In the deafening noise he shouted to those closest that they would all mount together and try to fight through the surround towards the river. Bloody Knife's warbonnet had attracted the attention of many hostiles; the warrior who could kill him would achieve a great "coup" for undoubtedly he was a renowned warrior. A trooper named Lorenz of Company M was standing close to the 'Ree, who was in turn beside Major Reno, who was shouting for the men to mount. Many of the soldiers did not hear the order, their backs being towards Reno, their hearing impaired by the clamour around them. Trooper Lorenz let out a cry and fell, obviously killed by a bullet intended for Bloody Knife. Two Cheyennes were concentrating upon the 'Ree. These were Crooked Nose and Turkey Leg. A bullet caught Bloody Knife squarely in the face and blew his head apart. A splash of blood and fragments of brain and flesh splattered over Major Reno, some striking him in the face. Reno yelled for the soldiers to mount then, while they were in process of obeying he called out for them to dismount. He was in the saddle himself at this time. Without another word he turned and charged across the clearing. Those of his men who were able then followed his example, but during the period of mounting and dismounting they had not returned the hostiles' fire and in consequence the emboldened Indians broke out into the clearing afoot and a-horseback and forced their way up close with devastating effect.

Among the whites still fighting in the clearing or surrounding timber was Lieutenant de Rudio, Charley Reynolds, several other scouts and about fifteen soldiers. These had not heard the order to withdraw nor seen it being obeyed. Also left in the woods were some half dozen Crows and Arikaris. Two of them, Goose and Young Hawk, tried to creep through the underbrush to join another Arikari, Forked Horn, who with two Crows, Half Yellow Face and White Swan, were firing at the hostiles who were closing in upon them. Discovered and cut off the two 'Rees then tried to get to a pair of horses tied among the trees. They got the animals untied and were mounting when Goose said: "I am hurt," and fell to the ground. A bullet had shattered his right arm. Another bullet killed the horse he had been mounting. Young Hawk leaned Goose against a tree, removed his soldier-coat, threw it aside and knelt beside Goose. Not far away valorous White Swan got on a horse and rode out alone to face the combined Sioux and Cheyennes, who withheld their fire while a large Cheyenne called Whirlwind urged his horse out in front to meet the Crow. Both warriors then charged at one another withholding their fire until the last moment. Their guns exploded almost simultaneously. Whirlwind fell off his horse dead; White Swan also fell off. After a moment he got on his hands and knees and tried to crawl back to his companions — who were howling a death-chant. His left hand had been shot off and one leg was broken. The enraged hostiles fired at him and Half Yellow Face ran to where Young Hawk squatted with Goose and asked him to give help in recovering the wounded man. Together they crept out, caught White Swan by the arms and dragged him into the safety of the underbrush. After this Young Hawk got on a horse and rode out into plain sight of the hostiles. They fired and missed; he returned the fire several times then withdrew into the timber again. When he dismounted he found Forked Horn pressing himself flat against the ground. Forked Horn was angry and indignant; he upbraided Young Hawk for drawing the Sioux fire; said that was not a sensible way to fight, for Young Hawk to go somewhere else and stand.

Among the soldiers Reno had deserted Lieutenant McIntosh, commander of G Company, perhaps more than any of the other soldiers and white scouts, could have felt irony; he was a white soldier, an officer — he was also a Mohawk Indian. While he was standing near Fred Girard and Charley Reynolds he heard the Indians step-up their howls and gunfire. Reynolds yelled something and ran towards a tied horse;

neither he nor McIntosh knew that the rest of the command had departed, was in fact, at that very moment bursting upon the Indians on the northeast side of the woods. Reynolds got into the saddle and spun the horse.

Beyond the trees near the river the Indians did not expect to see the soldiers charge out. When they emerged the hostiles quirted their horses frantically to get away, believing the soldiers were after them. When they eventually halted some distance off they saw that the soldiers were not pursuing them, but were trying to escape the surround.

Reno rode towards the river as fast as his horse would go. Those of his command who had followed were riding after him pell-mell. The Indians then returned and pursued their enemy and meanwhile other hostiles from the timber burst out on the far side and joined them, but the first party of hostiles being closer, closed upon the retreating soldiers faster. One of them fired an arrow at a soldier on a weak and lagging horse. It penetrated his head from front to rear. As the soldier was falling the Indian fired again. The second arrow struck the dead man in the shoulder before he fell into the water.

By this time Reno's fleeing men were in the river and the hostiles were among the hindmost. Farther back Charley Reynolds burst out of the timber. An Indian shot him off his horse but one foot hung up in a stirrup and he was dragged a ways. Lieutenant McIntosh led the remainder of the deserted men out of the woods and his horse collapsed under him with an arrow through its head. Trooper McCormick of Company G offered McIntosh his mount saying they were as good as dead anyway. McIntosh ran back to the protection of the trees followed by his companions. A little later he tried it again. By this time Reno and the balance of the command was lost to sight far ahead. Hostiles swarmed around McIntosh's band making for the river. On the banks several hostiles closed with McIntosh, pulled him from his horse and killed him. Most of those with him were also killed, a few were able to break clear and eventually catch up with Reno's detachment, others got back to the timber where they stayed until nightfall.

While Reno's men were crossing the river Indians among them managed to pull soldiers from their horses, knife, club, or drown them. Soldiers would turn and fire into the warriors from time to time but for the most part they made slight effort against the horde of Indians, concentrating instead upon urging their horses onward. Two Cheyennes got on either side of a trooper and quirted both man and horse making no immediate attempt to kill him. The soldier fended off their blows with a pistol in his hand which presumably the Indians thought was unloaded. Finally he turned and fired point-blank at one of the Indians, striking him in the chest. The other Cheyenne then struck the soldier over the head knocking him from his horse.

Lieutenant Varnum tried blasphemously to halt the panic, without success. Reno's men were forced by the hostiles towards the river where no crossing existed. It did not matter; they would force a crossing anyway. Three troopers got separated and went racing back the way they had come. There was no longer any discipline; any wish to aid or succour others; each trooper was bent only upon his own preservation. Three Cheyennes and two Sioux went after the escaping men. They were Cheyennes, Little Sun, Eagle Tail Feather, and She Bear. When they were about to overtake the soldiers — the two Sioux were farther behind — one of them swung abruptly away and spurred his horse towards a thicket of willows eastward, towards the river. The other two soldiers were apparently heading in the direction they had last seen Custer and his five companies. One of the horses began to fail badly; its rider then swerved and made for some timber. The two Sioux went after him. He was caught among the trees and killed. The last soldier, seeing some of the pursuit had gone after his companion among the trees, rode in a big arc seeking to get away westward. He finally got into a thicket of underbrush and timber several hundred yards ahead of the persevering Cheyennes. By the time the hostiles got up he had abandoned his spent horse and was forted-up behind a dead-fall with his carbine and pistol. Unable to escape and outnumbered he fought well until a warrior got around behind the dead-fall and shot him through the head. The man who killed him recited this story.

Back at the river where Reno's remnant strove to cross, the water was four feet deep. Indians on both banks shot at them. Many were content to sit on the bank watching and shouting encouragement to those of their comrades who plunged in after the troopers. Several warriors raced up shouting that Crazy Horse was coming. If any had noticed his absence since the fighting at the timber before the village it can be doubted if they wondered about it long for out in the river a big Sioux was brandishing a cavalry saber, knocking soldiers into the water with it, and the Oglala, Eagle Elk with a shiny new Winchester carbine was shooting into the backs of his enemies while his horse struggled to keep afloat. He killed at least three soldiers.

On the far bank a friendly was shot in such a way that he could not stand erect. He dragged his paralysed legs behind him into a thicket and there, propped up, continued to fire into the hostiles. When he was noticed several Sioux engaged him in a duel while others slipped around behind the thicket and shot him again. He tried to raise up and face those behind him but could not and one of the flankers ran up close and split his head with a rifle barrel. The others then came up and counted coup by plunging their knives into him. He was afterwards scalped and plundered.

On the near side of the river some Indian boys armed with bows were shooting arrows at a dismounted soldier who tried to dodge them and the fire which they had set to his hiding-place. He did not fire back; it was assumed he had either lost his guns or was out of ammunition. The Arikari Red Bear made it across the river where Major Reno was curbing his frantic mount among some of his soldiers. When the white men saw Red Bear they threw up their guns and the 'Ree began to shout: "Scout! Scout!" They did not fire at him. When he got up closer a sergeant handed him some cartridges from a broken box he was carrying. Some of the cartridges fell from the box and Red Bear got down to retrieve them.

Twenty-nine soldiers fell crossing the river. Reno had approximately ninety-odd men left from his original three companies. In the crossing Reno's adjutant — close friend of Lieutenant Varnum — Lieutenant Benjamin H. Hodgeson ("Benny") was shot through the thighs by the same bullet which killed his mount. A trooper sweeping by managed to grab Hodgeson from the water. Hanging to this soldier's stirrup Hodgeson was dragged up on to the opposite bank but when the soldier bent down to grab the officer, Hodgeson let go. The trooper went on. Hodgeson lay in the dirt firing at the Indians until killed.

The surgeon Doctor De Wolf made it across the river in company with his orderly, Clair, of K Company. He was riding slightly behind Clair up a narrow canyon towards the bluffs overhead which were Reno's destination, when a party of hostiles appeared abruptly in front of him. Soldiers which had attained the bluffs overhead saw both Clair and Doctor De Wolf killed and scalped.

The bank across the river where Reno emerged from the water arose quite steeply. The less panicked soldiers did not attempt to scale this rise although Major Reno and many men did; others rode up and down the bank seeking access routes via the innumerable gullies leading upward.

Reaching the plateau above many of the men were wounded, their horses exhausted. Not a few were afoot. Reno himself stopped on the ridge, still marked by the effluvia from Bloody Knife. One of the first men to reach the eminence was Lieutenant Varnum. He was still trying to calm the panic and halt the rout; his greatest ally was the spent condition of the horses. The men halted on the hilltop and Varnum immediately undertook to organise a nucleus of veterans to oppose the hostiles who, while still excited and eager, did not cross the river in great numbers. In fact a great many had by this time gone back to the timber or along the escape route to plunder the dead soldiers of apparel, weapons and ammunition. A few could be seen in the distance chasing loose cavalry horses. Varnum's efforts were rewarded when the troopers dismounted and lay down in defensive positions, many digging shallow pits for their bodies with pocket-knives, spoons, anything handy. The horses, which could go no further, were herded into the centre of the new position. Here the men of Reno's command prepared to make their last stand; here they made it.

The Indians, seeing the soldiers dismount, charged and were repulsed. Varnum tried to direct the gunfire and could not, the soldiers fired when and at what they fancied. They were fighting from instinct, many were seriously injured, nearly all were badly shaken. The volume of their fire more than the accuracy shattered a strong-heart attack launched frontally.

This type of combat had no appeal for Indians. Forted-up soldiers protected by heaps of saddlery, hardtack boxes, sufficiently dug-in to present minimal targets, firing downhill at exposed warriors who could not flank them — the only hill available was too far away — had an advantage over the hostiles which was both tactical and psychological. The Indians continued to fight, shout challenges to the few friendlies who had successfully completed the crossing with the soldiers, and harass them with long-distance gunfire, but after two or three charges the fighting dwindled, became a state of siege. In a manner of speaking this was fortunate for across the river, back in the trees, a great horde of hostiles were still seeking to destroy the small band of friendlies and soldiers there. When word arrived that the soldiers across the river had halted on the plateau, many warriors left the timber to reinforce their companions facing Reno.

One Indian back near the village did not share in the general exuberance. While he watched gleaners strip naked some thirty-two dead soldiers and friendlies, he did not believe this one small band of soldiers had attacked the huge Indian encampment without some purpose other than extinction. He listened to his nephew One Bull say that as far as he knew the Indians had lost seven Sioux warriors and one Cheyenne killed. He told his nephew to go back to the village of the Hunkpapas and stay there; to watch out for more soldiers. This was the chieftain Sitting Bull. He did not know at this time that the last and greatest triumph of his people against their white enemies was over; he did not know either, some say, that the fight against Reno was not the greatest victory of the day.

A badly shaken Marcus Reno was back in command upon the hill across the river. Varnum had resumed his subordinate position. The afternoon was spent, the sun going down in the west, but actually the fight had not taken as long as it takes to re-tell it. From the time Major Reno first stopped a quarter of a mile from the village to the time he retreated across the river, probably no more than thirty minutes was spent. Certainly not more than fifty minutes. The Indians, who reckoned time by the sun's movement said later there was no appreciable descent of the sun from the time the soldiers first opened fire on the village until they fled from the woods and crossed the river to the heights beyond.

A great many of the Indian leaders were content; they did not see much glory in sending the young men against Reno's position on the ridge. Most of the warriors themselves did not seek additional war-honours. Many rode up and down the field seeking wounded soldiers to kill and count coup upon. One Indian youth named Black Elk, who was fascinated by the whiteness of the stripped dead and dying, recounted in after years his impression that white men were very hairy; they not only had hair on their arms and legs, but even on their chests and some had hair down their backs. He was told to scalp a dying soldier by a warrior and when he started to take the wounded man's hair the soldier flopped about and ground his teeth so the lad shot him with his own pistol before completing the scalping.

Over by the timber a black-white-man was also dying. This was Isaiah Dorman, only Negro on the battlefield. He had a mortal wound in his chest and close by him an old Hunkpapa squaw squatted with a trade-musket — a smooth-bore — trained upon him. Dorman spoke *Lakota* fluently; he asked the old squaw not to kill him saying he was dying already. Sitting Bull came up shortly after two Sioux warriors arrived with the intention of stripping Dorman. The Negro asked the warriors not to count coup upon him until he died and while they were discussing this unusual episode Sitting Bull came up and recognised Dorman as a former resident among the Indians who had been known to them as Teat *(On Azinpi)*. He said Dorman was not to be killed, but permitted to die in peace. Water was brought, Dorman drank it and very shortly afterwards passed on.

Chapter Three

BEFORE Reno's remnant got to the heights a great many of the Indian women had struck their lodges preparatory to flight. Others had run away taking with them only the children and old people. Most had fled westward but not all; streams of wailing Indians were seeking refuge every which way. Some tipis had caught fire and burnt, others had been abandoned. When Sitting Bull rode back to the Hunkpapa camp-circle it was almost deserted. Meat drying racks had been knocked over, weapons and attire littered the churned ground, the half-wild Indian dogs wailed excitedly and loose horses were everywhere. The dust was thick and choking.

From the plateau across the river Reno's men had their first good look at the size of the encampment. It was then close to four o'clock and "time" which had consistently failed Reno all day long, now came reluctantly to his aid. Darkness would bring a measure of security. Indians did not voluntarily fight in the night, even victorious ones, those who did in this case found their aim impaired by darkness and limited vision. But from the hostiles' viewpoint there was no cause for anxiety. Reno was surrounded by "wolves" — scouts; because they frequently adorned themselves in wolfhides to achieve camouflage, the designation was appropriate. Reno, even after Benteen arrived, was at their mercy; the soldiers could not escape.

After sundown the soldiers could see thousands of little winking fires across the river, north and south. Lieutenant Gibson who was with Reno on the ridge wrote his wife (who was the sister of dead Lieutenant McIntosh's wife): ". . . Say nothing about what I am about to tell you, but if it hadn't been for Benteen every one of us would have been massacred. Reno did not know which end he was standing on, and Benteen just took the management of affairs in his own hands, and it was very fortunate for us that he did. I think he is one of the coolest and bravest men I have ever known. . . ."

Blunt, acrimonious Frederick W. Benteen, whose Civil War record was not outstanding, did indeed arrive in the nick of time. A large and sturdy man, leonine in appearance, of strong likes and dislikes totally lacking in tact but completely unafraid of man or devil, Benteen arrived on Reno's ridge hours after his disgust with Custer's orders encouraged him to disobey them and return to the valley of the Little Bighorn.

By the time he arrived Reno's demoralised command was in dire shape. The wounded had been made as comfortable as possible, their needs attended within the limits of unskilled ability. Some died that night. Beyond the circle were the Men Of War. Their calls and simulated owl-hoots kept the sentinels alert. Very few men slept. Where the officers crouched there was talk of Custer's failure to arrive. Among the enlisted men this was also the main topic. The night of the 25th was conducive to recollection; Custer had deserted his men on the Washita. He had failed his men at other times. There was a great deal of bitterness; a large amount of condemnation. No one attempted to excuse nor justify Custer's conduct. It was said he had seen the odds, had hurried away with the intention of rejoining Terry, and when two thunderous volleys of gunfire had been heard earlier no significance was attached to them for the valley had been filled with bedlam and gunfire. There was speculation regarding McDougall's detachment which when last seen had been escorting the packtrain. Ammunition and medicinals were in the packs. Of Benteen there had been no news since he had marched off with his three companies into the broken, jagged out-back country.

But Benteen had searched in vain for hostiles. "From my orders," he said, "I might have gone on twenty miles without finding a valley (with Indians in it). Still I was to go on to the next valley and if I didn't find any Indians I was to go on to the next valley. Those were the exact words of my order. . . . If I had carried them out I would have been twenty-five miles away. . . . As it was I was too far to co-operate with Custer when he wanted me. . . ." So Benteen defected from his orders. He rode far ahead of his "battalion" with Lieutenant Gibson and sent ten enlisted men even farther ahead as scouts. Arriving at a particularly eminent pinnacle he sent Gibson to its top for a study of the countryside. Gibson reported that he had seen nothing but broken and empty country as far as he could see; no signs of Indians anywhere. Benteen resumed the march and sent Gibson to different observation points from time to time. His reports did not vary; no Indians anywhere, just more broken and empty country ahead.

Benteen's patience was exhausted. He reversed the command and headed for the Little Bighorn Valley in the general direction of the river. Before he sighted Reno Creek he had described an immense horseshoe-shaped half-circling movement. His horses were thirsty and tired, his men no better off. His accomplishment had achieved little beyond convincing him that not even fleeing Indians would attempt to escape over the land he had just explored.

Striking the trail near Reno Creek where its namesake's command had ridden down the valley some time before, Captain Benteen ordered the men to rest and water their mounts. The ground was damp and soggy, slough-like, with ripgut and watergrass growing upon it. Here Captain Weir heard distant gunshots. Having watered his horse Weir mounted and loped away from the rest of the command. While the remainder of the "battalion" was making ready to leave, the first of the pack mules being protected by McDougall's B Company came down the trail with considerable anxiety. They were sweaty and dust-streaked. As Benteen's men drew their mounts away from the slough the mules hastened up and became bogged in the mud. Benteen did not wait to aid in extracting them; there were troopers from B Company as well as civilian packers in sight. Instead he led his command along the bank of the creek over the same trail Reno and Custer had made hours before. He arrived at the burnt tipi about four o'clock. About a mile beyond he came across Sergeant Kanipe of C Company on a lathered horse. Kanipe was carrying a message to McDougall at the slough to "hurry up with packs." Meaning the ammunition. Benteen told Kanipe about how far back McDougall was and continued down the valley. Still farther he met another rider. This trooper's horse was bleeding badly from the nostrils. The rider was John Martin, an immigrant boy from Italy who had been christened Giovanni Martini. Bugler Martin's command of English was so limited, his nature so warm and excitable he had been the pet of Benteen's own company for a long time. On detached service as orderly to Colonel Custer, Trooper Martin had a message for Captain Benteen from Custer's adjutant, Lieutenant W. W. Cooke — he of the glorious sideburns. This message was Ceorge Custer's last word to the outside world:

> "Benteen.
> Come on. Big village.
> Be quick. Bring packs.
>   P.S. Bring packs.
>   W. W. Cooke."

Trumpeter Martin described what he had seen as Benteen read the note. Reno, he said, was fighting in the valley before the village. (He may have been when Martin left Custer but by the time Benteen got Cooke's message he had fled across the river and taken the position upon the plateau.) Additionally, Martin said, after he had left Custer he was pursued by hostiles, his horse shot, himself shot at repeatedly. The Indians eventually gave up the chase and returned to their village. En route he had also met Boston Custer carrying a message to the packtrain.

While Martin talked gesticulating agitatedly Captain Weir and Lieutenant W. S. Edgerly rode up. Benteen showed them Cooke's message. They held a short conference after which Benteen ordered the column closed up, flankers out, and forward. He did not send anyone back to hasten the packtrain. Sergeant Kanipe and Boston Custer had presumably done this already.

Benteen's command rode at the lope as far as a hillock. By then they could clearly distinguish the thunder of gunfire and the howling of Indians. The dust was as thick as fog, but high, off the ground. From the knoll Captain Benteen got his first glimpse of the battlefield. He saw an overwhelming horde of mounted Indian warriors assaulting a small party of soldiers and friendlies trying to get to the river to cross it. This was de Rudio's party of survivors from the woods making their belated and final bid to reach the rest of Reno's command.

Indians were everywhere. They were not fleeing and amid the confusion it was hard to see that any of the tipis had been dismantled. In general the fighting warriors were riding in one of two directions. The hostiles attacking de Rudio were overwhelmingly superior in numbers and Benteen could not reach the defeated survivors no matter how hard he rode, before what appeared to be inevitable, overwhelmed them. He did not know whether the soldiers under attack by the river were from Reno's or Custer's command. He thought those men would never live to cross the river.

While Benteen was watching the fight near the river his attention was drawn to another development. Some of the Men Of War had seen his force ride up the hill. They now broke off from the attack at the river and formed into a separate war-party to attack him. Another group of Indians a short distance ahead and to his right were sitting perfectly motionless on their horses watching the fight at the river. These last had not seen Benteen's command arrive in their rear. K Company under Lieutenant Godfrey was ordered to charge them. It was then discovered that these were the Crows who had deserted Reno shortly after he had been halted before the village.

When he was within hailing distance Lieutenant Godfrey made a motion in the direction of de Rudio's detachment and yelled: "Soldiers?" The Crow leader shook his head and made a sweeping gesture with his arms indicating where Reno had been and where he now was atop the ridge; then he said: "Soldiers." Then the Crow made another gesture, this time off to his right, which Godfrey interpreted to mean more soldiers were in that direction.

Benteen's course was clear. He could hope to survive only if he avoided the obvious approach to the river which would involve an attempt to ride through the great mass of warriors towards de Rudio. This was patently out of the question with one hundred and fifty or so men. But if he rode northwest in a wide curve he might be able to get around Reno's hill across the river without too much jeopardy. He ordered his men to draw their revolvers. After this was done he led the command in a skirting manoeuvre around and through the broken, hilly country screening the valley proper — on the north — and made a fast ride for Reno's plateau.

The confusion and excitement down in the valley was so intense Benteen was able to complete most of his arc before being discovered by the hostiles. By then Reno's men saw him coming.

The Indians chased him but not in sufficient numbers to force a fight and when he finally arrived at Reno's hill the major ran out of the defensive circle and said: "For God's sake, Benteen, halt your command

and help me. I've lost half my men."

Benteen ordered his men to dismount and lead their horses into the circle. Reno, who was standing close to Benteen talking would break off in mid-sentence and fire his revolver. It was evident to Benteen that Marcus Reno and most of his men, including the heretofore relatively composed Lieutenant Varnum, were in the grip of a great demoralisation. Troopers were still arriving afoot, wounded and exhausted, from down along the river. One enlisted man walked to the edge of the circle with his carbine in one hand holding aloft a dripping scalp with his other hand and smiling broadly.

Lieutenant Hare of K Company approached Benteen with his hand out. While they were shaking hands Hare said: "I'm damned glad you got here. We got whipped like hell." Benteen appointed Hare acting-adjutant of the combined command and ordered him to take the strongest horse and ride to the packtrain with orders to make all speed to Reno's ridge.

Assuming command Benteen ordered an equitable division made of all available ammunition. He also re-aligned the men for defence. Some of Reno's troopers were completely out of ammunition, others had only a handful. The hostiles were still sniping but not in force. After Benteen's arrival the answering gunfire from the ridge discouraged all but the most valorous of the Indian warriors; after a time even these withdrew. It was at this time that the defenders could see a great body of warriors across the river racing down the valley. At a loss to understand the reason for this Benteen ordered the men to dig in, throw up everything in front of their positions which might turn an arrow or stop a bullet, and in all ways prepare for the return of the enemy.

The sounds of heavy and sustained gunfire arose from across the river. This seemed to end almost as abruptly as it had commenced. The warriors who still sniped at Reno's ridge appeared to be listening to this indication of another furious fight also. When they ceased shouting and shooting the soldiers on the plateau could hear the unmistakable din of battle. No one attempted to interpret what this meant and Captain Benteen, in council with Major Reno, showed the ranking officer Cooke's note. It was thought, if Custer was indeed still in the valley, he must soon come to their relief. A conversation ensued during which much speculation — and not a little condemnation — centred around Custer. It was felt that he more than likely had indeed left the valley, otherwise, seeing Reno's plight before the village, he would have hastened to his support. Since he had not, and since no one had seen him since he had sent Reno ahead to spearhead the attack, it now appeared very plausible he had not stayed to lend aid, but had taken the five companies and ridden to a juncture with General Terry.

It was suggested that perhaps he had retraced the route of march up Reno Creek. Benteen squelched that; his command and the packtrain as well had just come down that trail; there had been no sighting of the five companies. In the darkness before dawn another theory was advanced. Perhaps Custer had made a wide detour similar to Benteen's, so as to remain concealed as long as possible by the hills on the north side of the valley; had possibly crossed the river to take advantage of what skimpy cover the tree-fringe offered, and had gone around the ridge where Reno's command now huddled, so as to strike the hostiles farther to the north — which in fact was about what he had done.

While the night drew out an unexpected thing happened; Lieutenant de Rudio came walking into the soldier-circle. A little later one of the white scouts who had also been given up for dead, also came in. Still later, one by one, singly and in furtive groups two more civilians and thirteen soldiers, the last survivors from the band left behind in the timber, arrived. The last living white man was out of the valley, the *wasicuns* which remained were dead and mutilated, stripped naked, the tops gone off their heads.

But Indian dominance of the valley was to be short-lived, for the columns of Colonel Gibbon and General Terry, adhering to schedule, were approaching. In fact their dustclouds had been seen late in the afternoon and scouts sent to spy upon them, determine who they were and in what force they came. But the men on Reno's ridge knew nothing of this; nor did they know that of the six hundred and more men of the 7th Cavalry column which had ridden boldly down the Lodgepole Trail about noon, 25th June, 1876, only the men under Marcus Reno, Frederick Benteen, and McDougall's escort with the packtrain, were all that remained alive.

A reconstruction of Custer's last fight can be broken down into three phases. First; his action after Major Reno's detachment left him near the dead-warrior tipi. Secondly; Custer's subsequent actions, their presumed reasons and effects up to and including the firing of the final shot in his battle against the hostiles which vanquished him and five companies of the 7th Cavalry. Thirdly; his considerations for, and possible attempts to alleviate the condition of, the separated units of his divided command.

Every white man who rode with Custer was killed. There were no accredited survivors to recount what happened after he left Reno. Of his foemen there were many who, for a number of reasons, neolithic breast-beating and fear of reprisal being uppermost, told innumerable variations of the fight. Rarely did two coincide or even bear a similarity. Rain In The Face's story of having eaten the heart of Tom Custer has been quite thoroughly discredited. Gall, on the other hand, while conceivably motivated by a desire to deprecate his part in the battle, said truthfully that there was so much dust and confusion no one knew exactly what was happening. One of the best examples of conflicting testimony regards the killing of Colonel Custer himself; no less than four warriors claimed this distinction. But arbitrarily to brand all Indian versions of Custer's last battle false, as many historians do, is illogical, for the only survivors of the fight were Indians; only from their myriad stories could what actually occurred be reconstructed. Still, one must bear well in mind that no two Indians fought alike and very few knew what their comrades were doing ten feet away, therefore it is necessary to correlate all versions, plus the known location of the bodies and the route used for them to get where they fell, to present this famous and terrible slaughter with a degree of accuracy. Clearly, and with all other divergencies momentarily put aside, the *reason* for Custer deserting Reno was based in his deeply rooted personal belief in individuality. If he hadn't come to his death — and disgrace — on the Little Bighorn in 1876, he would have come to one or the other somewhere else; he was not a personally or militarily disciplined man, officer, or soldier. Those who failed to appreciate this aberration in 1876 — which did not include Sheridan, Sherman, Grant and others — came to know it in after years.

After Reno's detachment was lost to sight Custer followed his scouts to a knoll some distance away and there saw for the first time, the Indian encampment. By this time Reno was under attack at the south end of the village. The constant roar of gunfire was clearly audible. The scouts pushed on until they got a good look at the hostile encampment. Their previous estimation of the size was verified and brought to Custer's attention. He ordered the command to hasten. Riding along a wide ridge with the Crows out in front he came to a break in the terrain and halted there. While the scouts and soldiers were immobile, listening to the sounds of battle and straining to see, Custer and his brother Captain Tom rode ahead to another hillock from which they could see a number of hostile lodges, but the greater camp-circles were hidden by the timber and the bend of the river northward. Custer studied the village through field-glasses then turned and waved his hat at the rest of the column. Apparently he thought the village consisted of the tipis he had seen and no others. When his men galloped along the ridge the Indians saw them. A great many cried out in alarm and left the attack upon Reno to face this new threat which was materialising from the debouchment of Medicine Tail Coulee.

It was obvious to the hostiles that this new contingent of the enemy — they did not know whose command it was; those who thought about it at all considered it a part of Crook's command which had slipped around the Indian spies undetected. Many hostiles did not know for several days after the battle that Custer's force was an alto-gether different command.

The danger from Custer was obvious; with only a little luck he would be able to drive through the village before the Indians could gather in sufficient force to protect their people. So far the majority of warriors were still engrossed with Reno.

The Crows rode up a little hill from which they had a good view of the country down by the river. For the first time the attackers got a good look at the entire encampment.

Custer rode up this hill with Trumpeter John Martin after halting the column at the base of the hill. Moments later he went back down to join the command which had now progressed some three miles from where they had left Reno. Every soldier now held a gun in his hand cocked and prepared to fire. Here Colonel Custer detached Martin with the note to Captain Benteen. At this time some of the Crows started up a little band of hidden Sioux spies. In the erratic exchange of gunfire the warriors tried to frighten the troopers' horses by waving buffalo hides and raising the yell. In retaliation Custer ordered a fast advance. The Sioux fled towards the rider with E Company, the grey-horse troop, racing after them in the van of Custer's "battalion".

Allegedly "Mitch" Bouyer rode up to the Crow, Curly, at this point, gave him his field-glasses and told Curly to ride away; to seek a vantage point clear of the impending battle and watch. If the soldiers were going to be overwhelmed, Curly was to ride as hard as possible for General Terry's column and carry the news. After Curly left (there is another version of Curly's escape; about as believable as this one) Bouyer rode after Custer. The soldiers were aligned in company front, were riding at a trot over the treacherous shale towards the ford. When Bouyer came up Custer stopped and told him the Crows could leave; they had fulfilled their duty in guiding the column to the village. Bouyer told Custer he should leave also. While they were talking a hidden Sioux called to Bouyer — known to the hostiles as *Wica Nonpa* (Two Bodies), telling him to go back, to leave. When Custer urged his horse forward again Bouyer rode with him.

Custer's target was the northernmost village, that of the Cheyennes who by this time had gone in force to help the Hunkpapas four miles to the south. There were a few warriors on hand but not many. The old people, women and children, were standing around. The Cheyenne warrior White Elk lay in a lodge with a badly swollen thigh, result of a gunshot injury incurred against Crook on the Rosebud. Bobtail Horse, a renowned Cheyenne fighting man had not gone south; he had been trying to drill a hole through an elk tooth since early in the day. An elk's tooth was strong medicine; he did not intend to ride to battle until the hole was drilled so that he could affix the amulet in his hair. Shortly before Custer's unit swept into view he completed the drilling and tied the tooth into his scalp-lock. When he took up his old musket and went outside to catch his horse he saw a great line of soldiers riding towards the village and cried out: "Nutskaveho!" ("White soldiers are approaching!")

Roan Bear heard and ran up. An Oglala Sioux named White Cow Bull also heard. A Crazy Dog warrior called Calf who was painting himself for battle also ran up. While the excited warriors were shouting to one another an old Indian named Mad Wolf rode up. He exhorted the younger men against charging the soldiers; urged them to wait until someone could go after reinforcements. By this time the five Indians were mounted and riding towards the ford at the river where Custer's command would cross to strike the Cheyenne village. One of the warriors told the old man that it was a good day to die; that only the earth and the sky lasted for ever. Mad Wolf turned his horse towards the village and left them.

A fighting man named White Shield who had been down by the river now came riding up to join the four. He alone was armed with a bow and arrows, the others had rifles or carbines. On the Cheyenne side of the stream was a low ridge. Behind this the five Indians halted and prepared to make their stand. White Shield decided to ride down the river a short ways where his bow could span the distance better. By this time the soldiers were near the opposite bank.

When the four warriors behind the ridge began to fire and yell the soldiers slowed in their pursuit of the five Sioux spies they were chasing. This gave the strong-hearts time to cross the river where they joined the five Cheyennes. Custer's Crows had Spencer repeating carbines with which they peppered the ridge beyond which the embattled hostiles were hiding. The column halted across the river. Their near-side bank of the river offered no obstacle but across, where the hostiles were, the bank rose an abrupt thirty inches or so from the water. This conceivably caused Custer's hesitation; at any rate the one-sided duel went on for a time before the colonel waved for an advance into the water. He was in the lead when the troops splashed into the river and started across. By this time the gunfire was deafening. The soldiers had no idea how many hostiles were behind the ridge; the racket probably made it seem that there were hundreds instead of a short-dozen. Because the enemy gunfire kept them down, the hostiles were momentarily unable to raise up and fire. When they did not shoot most of the firing from Custer's column dwindled. During this very brief quietus Colonel Custer rode ahead with Bouyer on his left, an orderly carrying a guidon on his right. When the Crows were well out into the stream Goes Ahead heard a great ragged shout raised upstream from the charging column. He turned in time to see hundreds of hostile warriors breaking out of the willows along the river in a disorganised and headlong assault. Now the warriors behind the ridge raised up and fired into the nearest rank of soldiers. "Mitch" Bouyer and Colonel Custer were riding side by side firing at the exposed Indians on the ridge ahead of them. Without warning or sound Custer dropped his Remington rifle and fell from his horse in the shallow water with a bullet in the left breast. Bouyer slid off his mount, grabbed the dying officer and kept his head above water. The orderly carrying the guidon dropped it and collapsed. Another soldier riding past grabbed up the flag and pushed on. The Crows Hairy Moccasin, Goes Ahead, and White Man Runs Him, turned and fled after witnessing the fall of Colonel Custer.

Custer's fall caused a moment of demoralisation among the soldiers nearest him but the troopers farther back were firing in volleys into the ridge and the watching hostiles beyond were compelled to take cover once more. All they saw was the white officer fall into the river from his sorrel horse; the 'breed Bouyer dismount to aid him. They did not know who the officer was.

The hostile reinforcements rendezvoused with the ten warriors behind the ridge. Against their massed fire the exposed and floundering soldiers were helpless. After Custer's fall they began to fall back, to withdraw towards the far bank down which they had ridden moments before. White Cow Bull the Oglala said the soldiers seemed to lose spirit, become confused, entangled with each other and their dripping, frenzied horses. They made it back to the bank — those not shot in midstream — and there they tried to make a stand but the mass of warriors opposed to them, which was being steadily increased as more war-parties raced up, ultimately compelled them to continue their retreat towards the slopes of Medicine Tail Coulee. Their intention may have been to reach the ridge but by this time they were surrounded by angry hordes of Indians.

When the Indians charged back across the river the ten warriors leading were those which had originally caused the soldier-column to halt at the ford. Riding with White Cow Bull was a Ute named Yellow Nose, next to him the son of chieftain Ice. The latter was yelling a war-chant when a bullet knocked him from his horse. The soldiers were having trouble with their horses. While the trooper with the guidon was fighting to control his mount Yellow Nose raced in and snatched the little flag from his grasp. As he rode away he struck another soldier with the guidon, counting a coup.

He escaped without injury. Some of the soldiers gave up trying to control their horses and let them go. This inspired the Indians to shout that the soldiers were fleeing; they then charged but the soldiers were standing their ground and when the Indians came close a fierce volley dropped some and drove the others back.

Another charge was mounted, again the hostiles were repulsed. A Cheyenne strongheart called Backward Belly charged into the defenders with such ferocity he forced several soldiers to relinquish hold of their horses; these fled through the ranks rearward.

Because Custer's command had been somewhat spread out in riding down Medicine Tail Coulee, Companies I and L — both riding bay horses — had been in the rear when the force struck the river. They were therefore farthest back when the retreat was undertaken after Custer's fall and the arrival of the hostiles in force. In command was Captain Myles Keogh riding his horse Comanche. Keogh led his companies to a ridge overlooking the river. The other companies, F, C, and E, mounted respectively on bay horses, sorrels and greys, and under the command of Captain George Yates, withdrew to the western slope of the same ridge. They were for the most part dismounted. Their confusion and demoralisation did not prevent them from fighting an instinctive delaying rear-guard action until they got part way up the slope.

It appears that both commands tried to reach a pinnacle (where the battlefield monument now stands) and affect a juncture. Had they been able to accomplish this their position would have been similar to Reno's on the ridge across the river four miles to the south, and if they had there is reason to believe they might, like Reno, have survived. But this is based on the fallible premise that the Indians would not have tried to prevent such a meeting, which in fact they were fighting fiercely *to* prevent.

The hostiles now arrayed against Custer's column were in overwhelming numbers. Gall had arrived with a party of Hunkpapas, Sansarcs and Minniconjous, to prevent the juncture. Crow King with more Hunkpapas and some Blackfeet Sioux charged up from the east. Brave Wolf with a powerful force of vengeful Cheyennes struck from the left. Tom Custer's company had George Custer with them; no one can say whether he was dead or dying at this time. At any rate he was borne along with the soldiers and the battle became a series of mêlées. It was enough for an Indian war-leader to set an example for his warriors; there was very rarely any strategy to an attack or a battle. Indians fought as individuals, each seeking

135

to achieve war-honours, count coup, capture horses and weapons. Killing an enemy was naturally desirable, but of much greater importance was the striking of an enemy with one's hands or weapons while he was still alive, and riding away unscathed; this was the greatest feat of all — and well it might be for few warriors were successful at it.

Crow King's war-party charged L Company and a warrior in the foremost rank named Rain In The Face, who was riding a good buckskin horse, had the mount shot from under him. He managed to dodge the hooves of those coming after and get away unscratched. A big Cheyenne dressed in robes made from mountain lion pelts charged individually. For a while his comrades raced after him but when the soldiers fired a volley the others veered off. The Indians howled encouragement and prayers for the Cheyenne. It seemed incredible that he could live through such a barrage of bullets. He rode up to the soldiers and made several tight little circles then turned and rode back to his friends, opened his robe and let several bullets fall out. He was what was called a Holy Man, immune to bullets. There were several instances of other miracles on the field that day, but from the Indians' standpoint the most unexpected and unusual episode occurred when the soldiers of E Company turned their grey horses loose and undertook to charge upon the Indians afoot. Witnesses said the troopers shot wildly and made motions with their arms in the air. The Indians in front fell back swiftly then they charged. The soldiers made no concerted defence. One who rode down the hill on his horse behind the men afoot was shot through the chest by Iron Hawk. He emitted a scream and grabbed the forks of his saddle, the horse bearing him along. Iron Hawk rode after him, knocked him out of the saddle and dismounting beside him, brained the soldier with his bow.

Quite a number of the Cheyenne squaws were now trying to catch the grey horses. Bolder squaws and youths were upon the fringes of the battle seeking plunder or dead soldiers to strip and mutilate. Colonel Custer's brother-in-law Lieutenant James Calhoun and his entire E Company did not require ten minutes to kill after they abandoned their horses and fled down the ridge into the Indians. Their loss left a fatal gap in Custer's line. The bay-horse company, L, was now faced by a formidable press of warriors which completely surrounded it; cut it off from I Company. The soldiers fought desperately but unavailingly. As in the case of E Company the Indians fired a simultaneous and deafening volley which all but annihilated L Company. These were very likely the two volleys Reno's survivors reported hearing; the first volley marked the passing of Calhoun, the second marked the vanquishment of Myles Keogh and L Company.

In a slight depression on the sidehill I Company was the next to receive the hostiles' attack. It was also overcome and wiped out. In each instance it can be doubted that the individual battles did not consume more than two or three minutes. Despite subsequent manhandling of the corpses they were found to be generally in a loose but military formation. In the case of I Company the fight was said to have lasted less than two minutes. When the Indians swept over Keogh's contingent they did not pause before attacking I Company.

F and C Companies were still resisting. For the most part the men were dismounted. The route up the hill towards the ridge was marked by dead and dying soldiers. They had almost reached the eminence when some thousand Sioux under Crazy Horse charged them from the security of a gully. At the same time Cheyennes under Two Moon charged over the ridge and down along the columns' flank. The soldiers were thus unable to reach the ridge. Hostiles above fired down into the ranks and those of Two Moon's company attacked the flank and wings. A few soldiers attempted to mount and break out of the surround. They were unsuccessful. By this time a mounted man was doomed, the Indians were close, their fire directed primarily at the best targets. The troopers now fought from the ground. There was an Indian who did not dismount. This was Soldier Wolf. He rode towards a trooper who snapped his carbine, it did not go off. Soldier Wolf rode the soldier down. As he was passing the trooper got up and tried a second time to kill him. Soldier Wolf shot and killed the trooper.

Finally ground to a standstill by the Indians, Custer's 7th Cavalry remnants were under such ferocious attack, so knocked from normal alignment, many were forced to fight individually as the Indians did. But few hostiles who were in close trying to count coups accounted for many soldiers; most of the kills were made by Indian snipers beyond the dusty, brawling mêlée. The Oglala, Long Elk, was astride his horse riding aimlessly with blood pouring from his mouth. A warbonneted Hunkpapa was duelling with a soldier. He would raise up and fire and drop flat. Once when he raised up a bullet caught him squarely in the face. Some Indian boys nearby watching were terrified by his flopping and ran away. Another Sioux stood bent over with no lower jaw. A lance-bearing Arapaho came riding up into the thickening dust and bedlam. Nearby was a wounded Sioux warrior trying to get to his feet. He was very close to the soldiers. The Arapaho charged him, lanced him through the chest and killed him. Apparently the Arapaho thought the Sioux was one of the Crows or 'Rees. Some Sioux bucks standing near saw this happen; they were furious and turned to kill the Arapaho. When the Arapaho saw what had happened, how angry and vengeful the Sioux were, he turned his horse and ran away.

The warrior White Bull urged Crazy Horse to lead a party of warriors into the soldier-circle. When the Oglala refused White Bull rallied the hostiles and led them. Passing a soldier who fired at him White Bull grabbed the man and pulled him to the ground where he killed him. Crazy Horse who was behind came up and counted the second coup on the dead soldier. Four mounted soldiers tried to make a run for it. Three were overtaken by mounted warriors and killed. The fourth got a good start and maintained it. His horse was strong and fast, the Indians' horses were worn from the long, fast ride from the fight four miles southward; the soldier was escaping. All but two warriors gave up the chase and returned to the battlefield. Then the soldier drew his revolver and shot himself. (Some authorities believe this was Lieutenant Harrington of C Company; others say the man was *shot in the back* when they found him; clearly it would be very difficult for a man to shoot himself there.)

Here, with the hostiles swarming upon them, in most cases no more than arms' length away, the 7th Cavalry detachment under Colonel George Armstrong Custer made its last fight amid the deafening clamour with dust choking-thick, the scream of gutted horses and mangled men and the yells of nearly two thousand Indians around them. Horses with arrows sticking out of their bodies, maddened by fear and agony, trampled Indians and soldiers alike. In a gully a small party of soldiers were making a determined stand. Indian snipers could not see them among the smoke, dust, and underbrush, well enough to wipe them out. They were generally reluctant to charge into the gully. Dropping arrows in an arc wounded some of the soldiers but did not materially hinder their firing into the Indians who approached too close. Two warriors rode their horses straight into the gully. When one seemed reluctant the other struck his horse to urge him forward. A soldier leapt up to fire at them. One of the Indians struck him with a clubbed musket. Two more soldiers came out of the underbrush but the Indians were too close, they were knocked over by the charging horses. Three soldiers then came out of the gully behind the braves. One of the Indians swung his clubbed gun and unhorsed a soldier, the other leapt at the man nearest him with his knife. The third soldier fired just as his horse bolted, unseating him. The remaining mounted Indian slid to the ground but his horse had become wild with panic and for a moment he could not control him; when he was finally able to calm the beast he went over where the white soldier and his friend were rolling in mortal combat. The knife-wielding warrior cut the soldier's throat as his companion came up; there was no longer need for assistance, but when the warrior bent to help his friend up, he collapsed. Until then the Indian did not see two gaping wounds in his comrade, who was dying; in fact expired as his friend held him. Mounting, the remaining Indian raced up the gully and emerged at its head on to the flat land above. There he abandoned his own horse and caught a fine soldier-mount which he used during the remainder of the battle.

By this time what cavalry horses had not been released by their owners or holders, or stampeded by the Indians, had been shot by the soldiers for use as bulwarks. Behind these arrow-studded carcasses soldiers continued to fight. The tumult was beyond description, the din greater than anything the Indians had ever seen or participated in before. Warriors, in describing what they saw and did during that time in after years, seemed fairly unanimous in their opinion that the fight did not last more than twenty-five minutes, and probably lasted no more than twenty minutes after the retreat from the river. Much of the fighting was hand-to-hand, all of it was desperate and without quarter.

The Sioux, White Bull, had his horse shot from under him. He charged upon a nearby soldier afoot. The soldier aimed his carbine at White Bull but it did not fire. (After the battle many of the 7th Cavalry's weapons were found to be jammed by expanded and defective ammunition; this may have been one of them.) When White Bull continued to run towards the soldier he threw the weapon at the Indian and closed with him. The soldier was unexpectedly strong and courageous, he tried to seize the warrior's gun and almost succeeded. White Bull clung to the weapon out of desperation. The soldier then beat him with his fists and White Bull managed to slash the soldier in the face with his quirt. The soldier let go of the gun but only for a moment, then he grabbed the warrior again, and once more White Bull struck him with the whip. Now the soldier began to pummel the Indian with his fists. White Bull was being hurt and could not protect himself. The soldier suddenly seized his hair and pulled White Bull's face close (the Indians said to bite off his nose; more than likely his intention was to break his neck or knock him unconscious with a blow to the jaw). White Bull then commenced howling for help. Two hostiles who were passing by heard his screams and went to his rescue. In their attempts to strike the soldier they repeatedly struck White Bull. Finally however they managed to stun the soldier. White Bull then leapt free and struck the soldier with his carbine, knocking him down. All three Indians counted coup on the vanquished soldier.

Another Sioux, coming upon a prone soldier beside a dead hostile, fired an arrow into him. The soldier leapt up with a great cry and began to run. A second arrow killed him.

The survivors of C and F Companies were dwindling, their fire lessening. A small group on a hillside completely surrounded and infiltrated by hostile warriors, their end was rapidly approaching. The Indians made many conflicting claims about the valour of the white soldiers in general, but none denied that the last soldiers to be killed fought valiantly. They were exposed to fire from every side, their only cover was behind dead horses and dead comrades. The final charge upon this band was led by a Cheyenne named Bearded Man who was shot and killed only a few feet from where the last few white survivors lay.

Gunfire slackened. From the hills around the battlefield hundreds upon hundreds of Indian spectators sat; old men, squaws, young boys. Desultory gunfire continued, irregular and not always close. A white soldier, tall and broad, suddenly leapt to his feet upon the sidehill and ran towards a gully. Upon its edge before plunging down, he halted. Below were hundreds of waiting warriors. The soldier put his pistol to his head and pulled the trigger. Back in the shambles of the dead-horse circle Indians crept in close to find soldiers who were not yet dead. One warrior came upon a dying trooper and leapt upon him. The soldier saw the descending knife and cried out: "Don't John," or: "Oh, John!" The Indian killed him. The name "John" was a frontier colloquialism used to address male Indians. The warrior was subsequently known as John.

Another individual display occurred back down by the river where a Sergeant Butler (L Company) who had been mortally wounded before the final retreat and who may have recovered consciousness only at this time, got to his feet and began firing his pistol at Indians nearby who were greatly surprised to find this man, covered with blood and who had been presumed dead, yet alive. Because to kill so brave a foeman was a great coup many warriors mounted their horses and rode towards him. He held them at bay until his ammunition was exhausted then a rifle ball felled him. The Indians who had fought him said he was the bravest man among the white soldiers.

The killing of the wounded did not take long. Two fat squaws knelt beside a bloody soldier and removed his clothing. When one then undertook to remove the soldier's genitals with her knife he leapt up and jumped at her. The old squaws were properly horrified and began to yell. A younger woman working close by ran up and stabbed the soldier from behind killing him. A soldier with captain's insignias lying on the hillside near the dead-horse barricade quite unexpectedly propped himself up on one arm and looked about. He had a black moustache which curled upwards at the outer edges and a short black beard. Seeing Indians bludgeoning the dying and looting the dead around him he attempted to raise his pistol. A warrior close by who had witnessed this resurrection leapt upon the dying man, wrenched his pistol away and shot him in the face with it. Other Indians then came up and counted coup on the captain, who may have been Myles Keogh.

Sitting Bull arrived on the field about this time and when informed all the soldiers were dead he ordered the Indians to leave them, to go away, not to plunder them any more. Some obeyed, most did not; the acquisition of good guns and ammunition was a powerful incentive to remain.

The shadows were lengthening, there was a strong odour in the air; gunpowder, blood, bloating horses, death. It was not a healthy place to stay; the afternoon was hot and still.

Some warriors still sought war-honours and rode southward where Reno and Benteen were dug-in upon the hill across from the main village.

The camps were full of excited people; warriors rode back and forth, squaws carrying uniforms, pieces of horse-gear, trudged towards their lodges. Young Indian boys hurried here and there with bows and arrows seeking soldiers to shoot; some had soldier-scalps on sticks which they waved with pride. The Brûlé chieftain's wife Woman Who Walks With The Stars went down along the river seeking stray cavalry horses. These were much prized for aside from being big and strong and valuable, they frequently had personal effects of worth tied behind the saddles. In the underbrush not far from the stream she came upon a crawling soldier. He had a carbine with which he was trying to get to the water. He was mortally wounded. She watched his agonised progress for a while then picked up a tree limb and crept forward. At the water's edge he saw her and tried to cry out. She ran up and struck him over the head with the limb. He sank into the water. She kept on striking at him.

Wounded warriors straggled to the camp-circles from the Custer battlefield. From the north came more injured. Some were laid out on robes to die, others, less seriously hurt, sat in the shade and recounted their war-honours. There was a lot of talk. Braggarts were derided, heroes extolled, liars greeted with scorn and laughter. Much had happened; it would be many days before it was all told, years before wheat and chaff were separated. Several warriors said they were standing not ten feet away and saw Colonel George Custer shoot himself. They said he raised his pistol while with the soldiers on the hillside and shot himself in the temple. Credence was given this tale by the relief column which arrived on the field the next day; Custer was lying naked, his arms flung out across the bodies of two other dead soldiers. He had a bullethole in his left breast and one in his temple. Nearby was Captain Tom Custer of C Company. Not far from Tom Custer lay adjutant, Lieutenant Cooke, with part of his face missing. Lieutenant Algernon Smith was lying on his side as though in slumber. Captain George Yates was on his back. Enlisted men were clustered in small groups. Nearly every man was stripped and many had been split from thigh to ankle with an incision cut diagonally across the ankle severing the Achilles tendon so that soldier-spirits could not chase Indian-spirits in the Hereafter. For a distance of over a mile the soldier-corpses were "strewn like seeds cast from a sower's hand" as a witness said. Most had been yanked one way and another by looters taking their arms, clothing, personal effects. Captain Keogh was not violated; Indians seeing the Agnus Dei about his neck feared reprisal for mutilation by this white-man medicine. Calhoun was not far from Keogh.

Where they found Custer were the most bodies; behind or close by the horse-barricade. Accounts differ as to the exact number of men who died with Custer. Some say two hundred and six, others estimate the number as high as two hundred and twenty-five men. Custer's strength after detaching Benteen and Reno was approximately two hundred and twenty-five men. This does not include Indian allies. The relief columns' accounts differ nearly as much as Indian accounts. Counting friendlies the highest account must be at least ten men too low.

In the matter of the soldier who shot himself when outdistancing Indian pursuers (possibly Lieutenant Harrington), there were several versions. The Crow, Curly, said he watched this race from his hillside. He said the soldier was making good his escape; that all but two of the Sioux abandoned the pursuit when they saw how strong and fast the soldier's horse was. That the two Sioux who persisted finally reined up; one threw up his rifle and shot at the soldier, but missed him. Then, Curly said, the soldier did an astonishing thing: he put his pistol to his head and pulled the trigger. (This man's grave has never been marked.) Another version is this: Curly, so-called sole survivor of the Custer "massacre," waited until the last Sioux pursuer turned back then rode down the hill and intercepted the soldier, who, seeing still another Indian after him, urged his horse to greater efforts. Curly then raised his gun and shot the soldier in the back, killing him. Old Indian scout Herb Record who had a cabin on the banks of the Little Bighorn River and who died a few years ago, said he knew this version of the killing to be the truth; that he and Trooper Ford, a participant in Reno's rout, afterward located and buried this soldier.

Another much-publicised factor alleged to have contributed greatly to the soldiers' defeat was the matter of jammed guns. Some Indians said they had seen soldiers hacking at expanded cartridges with knives and stones, implying faulty ammunition. Undoubtedly this did happen, but if it had been as prevalent as some authorities contend, why did not Reno or Benteen remark upon it at the courts of inquiry convened later; their men were armed with the same guns and ammunition Custer's command had.

Mutilation occurred. Members of the relief column said it did not. One warrior, while leading his horse among the vanquished seeking war-trophies came upon a dead officer with the most unique whiskers he had ever seen. This was of course Lieutenant Cooke, the adjutant. The Indian fleshed-off one cheek and the chin, tied his trophy to an arrow and carried it in his hand as he sought additional mementoes. Farther on the warrior came upon the partially concealed body of a scalped Indian. This man he recognised as Lame White Man the Cheyenne war-leader. He had not been present when Lame White Man had been shot by a warrior who mistook him for an Arikari; who scalped him?

The Cheyenne, Bobtail Horse found a

whisky flask upon a soldier. He drank it empty assuming it to be a very potent white-man medicine. When the whisky hit his stomach he was compelled to vomit. He told his companions that while soldier-medicine had great and indisputable "power" it was very bad medicine for Indians.

In the Sansarc encampment a small party of freshly-arrived Indians were being surrounded and held prisoner by the agitated Sioux who accused them of being friendlies. They were going to kill them all when a Cheyenne passing by on his way to the seige at Reno's hill, rode up. He told the Sansarcs they were holding Little Wolf a prominent although elderly Cheyenne warrior, who was chieftain of the band with him. The Sansarcs then made sarcastic reference to the safety and lateness of Little Wolf's arrival and he told them that while en route to the Little Bighorn Valley he had unexpectedly come upon a great body of soldiers near the Rosebud. These soldiers, he said, were between his band and the valley and knowing he would be killed if discovered Little Wolf hid his party after sending out "wolves" to watch the soldiers. But the soldiers were making towards the valley and Little Wolf could not get around them, he therefore had to trail after them and could not get up to the main hostile camps until after the soldiers had attacked. Except for Little Wolf's recital history might have accepted Custer's belief, before parting from Benteen and Reno, that the Indian sign seen *behind* the column was made by hunters from the main village.

After "Custer and five companies (were) wiped from the face of the earth," as newspapers were to say shortly, and the triumphant warriors had either returned to their villages or gone on upriver to join the seige of Reno and Benteen, the survivors across the river made a sortie. It happened this way: When the two echoing volleys of gunfire had been heard by the men on Reno's ridge, Captain Weir said to Lieutenant Edgerly: "That must be Custer." Weir then stood up straining to see southward but the dust obscured vision. He then said: "I'm going to ask them," meaning Reno and Benteen, "but if they won't go, will you take D Company and come along?" Edgerly replied: "Yes."

Captain Weir went to Major Reno with the suggestion that the command be moved southward in order to assist the men he assumed were fighting Indians there. Reno refused to move and Weir argued with him. Reno was adamant. Weir then took his horse and rode northward beyond the ridge and Lieutenant Edgerly, assuming he had Reno's permission, mounted D Company and went after him. Indians south of the plateau watched Weir and Edgerly but did not attack them in force. They proceeded about three-quarters of a mile along the broken hilltops until they had a good view of the valley, northward. They saw a towering mushroom of dust and thousands of Indians milling around. It appeared that many of the hostiles were shooting into the ground. It was possible to make out a blue uniform now and then but these were among the Indians, acting in consort with them and therefore had to be hostiles attired in army blouses.

In the absence of Weir and Edgerly the packtrain came up after having followed in general the route taken by Custer but staying closer to the screening rim of the hills above the valley and across the river. Evidently they escaped mass-attack only because the hostiles were occupied with Custer; they did fight off several small attacks before reaching Reno's hill. Indian accounts later attributed the packtrain's safe arrival on Reno's plateau to the fact that the hostiles did not know how strong the attackers were nor in what manner they arrived in the valley.

After the packtrain's arrival most of Reno's command mounted and followed after Weir and Edgerly. No one yet suspected what had happened to Custer. Lieutenant

Wallace said: "After we occupied the hill there was no uneasiness about Custer: but there was a great deal of swearing about General Custer running off and leaving us. . . ." Edgerly said: "Nobody had any idea that Custer was destroyed. The belief was general that he had gone to join Terry." Lieutenant Varnum said: "I suppose everybody felt as I did, wondering what had become of Custer and where he was. I don't know that there was any special worry — he had five companies with him. . . ."

In recalling the night of the 25th on the hill Lieutenant Godfrey said: "There was an impression among the men that Custer had been repulsed and had abandoned them." Frederick Benteen had a similar viewpoint: "It was the belief of the officers on the hill during the night of the 25th," he said, "that General Custer had gone off to join General Terry and that we were abandoned to our fate."

Of course by the time Weir, Edgerly and the others got to the hill where they stopped, Custer, his brother Tom, Adjutant Cooke, Custer's brother-in-law Calhoun, Myles Keogh, the 7th's commandant's son Lieutenant Sturgis; all men of the five companies were dead.

In moving after Weir and Edgerly Reno's men had to carry the wounded with them. This delayed the juncture of both contingents until after six o'clock. Benteen who was in the van saw Indians mounting their horses down in the valley and riding towards them. Additionally, warriors were streaming back southward from the vicinity of the Custer battlefield in great force. (This was after Sitting Bull had ordered them to desist.) The hostiles which had been watching the slow and painful advance of Reno's command, emboldened by the appearance of reinforcements, began firing at the soldiers. It was apparent these Indians were better armed than they had been earlier. There was no defensive position closer than the one the column had abandoned; orders were passed to withdraw back the way they had come. Reinforced by McDougall's pack-train-escort, amply provisioned with ammunition, the soldiers fought a successful action until back to the pits at Reno's ridge. There the Indians made a spirited frontal attack and the battle became general and intense.

Casualties among the men were slight but among the unprotected horses and mules they were heavy. With his reinforced command Reno was able to fight off the Indians' best efforts. They withdrew then and undertook to shoot arrows so that they would drop among the soldiers; they also sent sniping parties of strong-hearts creeping up the hill, but these were driven back with no great effort and ultimately the attack was called off. Most of the Indians went down the hill and across the river to their villages where burial ceremonies were under way. Dead warriors were adorned in their finest raiment, faces painted, weapons lashed beside them upon burial platforms, war-horses led up and shot to provide the spirit with transportation, and the dead were then ushered out of this world and upon their long journey to the Sand Hills. There was the customary wailing and penitentially self-inflicted injuries; breasts slashed, fingers cut off, bodies gashed with knives.

The wounded were attended by medicine-men whose knowledge regarding the care for bullet wounds was sound. All these things followed a set pattern. When the dead were "buried" the camps always moved. In this case, with the soldiers still alive atop the hill across the river, the tradition must be followed. In several of the camps this was emphasised by the reports of "wolves" who reported more soldiers approaching the valley; but this knowledge was not possessed by all the camps.

The matter of Indian casualties is open to debate. The Northern Cheyennes said they lost six killed. These were: Black Bear, Hump Nose, Lame White Man, Limber Bones, Noisy Walking and Whirlwind. The

Sioux allegedly lost twenty-nine warriors including: Young Black Moon, White Buffalo Bull, Young Bear, Young Skunk, Deeds, Black Fox, Bear With Horns, Bad Light Hair, Dog With Horns, Chased By Owls, Dog's Back Bone, Cloud Man, Elk Bear, Flying By, Hawk Man, Kills Him, Guts, Plenty Lice, Red Face, Swift Bear, Standing Elk, Swift Cloud, White Eagle, and Three Bears.

Twenty-nine Sioux and six Cheyennes. (It is the author's belief that this complete list of Indian casualties has never before appeared in print.) Among the Sioux there is an old deerskin enumerating each dead warrior by sign-painting. There is also another memento; inscribed upon another tanned hide is the name of the warrior the Indians say rushed up and shot Custer in the temple after he was found dead. This was held to be a shameful thing; coup had already been counted on Custer. This man's name cannot be made public; he bore his disgrace to his grave and his descendants are ashamed of his act.

Of all the questions posterity asks of this battle the outstanding one concerns the great disparity in casualties. By Custer's orders the soldiers were rationed one hundred rounds apiece before they rode to battle. By the time Reno's men got across the river and atop the ridge many were out of bullets; when Benteen came up he ordered his men to divide their cartridges with Reno's men. During the fight before the Hunkpapa village the soldiers were a quarter of a mile from the village; they fired constantly at it and the densely packed ranks of hostiles all around them. Afterwards, atop the ridge and reinforced by Benteen, and eventually McDougall and the packtrain, the battle continued. Assuming the soldiers were demoralised, incapable of accuracy, it seems incredible that they did not kill more warriors than reported.

Custer's five companies on the other hand — or roughly two hundred and thirty men — did not live long enough to exhaust their ammunition, but they fought as long as they were able and jammed-guns aside, must certainly have gotten off at least two rounds apiece on the average. (Assuming Calhoun's and Keogh's men did not, the last companies to die certainly got off *more* than two rounds.) Again, the soldiers were firing into massed Indians.

It has been stated and probably correctly that a large percentage of the soldiers fired at random, in the air, erratically — *but they fired;* some of the warriors related long after the battle that some soldiers shot themselves and each other; few will deny that this very likely happened, but still *the soldiers fired their pieces.* Again, although some warriors claimed the troopers indulged in mass-suicide, one can find ample reason for doubt; Reno's men were in equally bad straits as Custer's; none of them recounted suicide among their comrades.

In the end there seems no shortage of accounts attesting to the fact that the soldiers used their guns against the masses of hostiles. Granting the 7th Cavalry was made up of about forty per cent recruits whose aim was faulty, six hundred men firing repeatedly in a battle which lasted most of an afternoon — Reno's, Benteen's and McDougall's commands at least — even under the most adverse of conditions would normally account for more than thirty-five foemen. It seems highly improbable that a hundred veteran Indian fighters with about one hundred rounds apiece did not kill a single Indian.

In all that confusion at least one Indian was killed by his allies through error; this need not have been the only such incident. In conclusion it appears very likely that the Indians minimised their casualties. Some years back an old man offered to show the author three mummified warriors secreted in a cave which were casualties of the Battle of the Little Bighorn; their names are not listed among hostile casualties. How many like them were hidden away — remain so to this day? No one will ever know.

The matter of mass-suicide among the soldiers can be explained by the fact that fatally wounded white men *did* kill themselves during the Indian wars, and not exclusively upon the Custer battlefield, to escape being hacked apart by coup-counting warriors or vengeful squaws.

Consider two more factors: Custer's companies in their flight from the river were surrounded by Indians. Regardless of the direction they fired in, there were Indians. Again, Reno's men fought largely afoot when they dismounted facing the village and later in the woods. They were firing at Indians. If, in both instances, soldier-marksmanship had been so faulty the Indians would have perceived it; would have charged and overwhelmed the attackers. That they indicated respect for the accuracy of Reno's fire at least indicates the marksmanship was somewhat telling upon them. Atop the ridge after the juncture of Reno's force with Benteen's, the soldiers whose aim — and nerves — was proven undependable, were withdrawn from the firing line and relegated to loading guns for those in the line whose hands were steadier.

In deceiving the enemy concerning casualties the hostiles did only what all soldier-races have always done; given the foe as little comfort as possible. If on the other hand the Indians lied, as the whites said they did, at least this was not their exclusive prerogative. An example of white-American prevarication appeared in the *Rapid City Black Hills Journal* two years after the battle, under the dateline of 13th July, 1878. This quoted a supposed recitation by Sitting Bull:

"The people of the United States blame me for having killed Custer and his army. They came to attack me in sufficient numbers to show that they wanted to destroy me and my children. For three days I looked at them coming towards me. I then assembled the young men and told them to put up the oldest tepees and build fires inside and outside them. Put blankets and other things on sticks and stick them around the fires, so they would look like people. In the meantime I sent the women and children across the hills to safety. I then turned around two or three bluffs with my soldiers. I gave Custer time to arrive and commence firing on the empty tepees. When he did I fell upon him by the rear and in less than two hours destroyed him. When I saw them coming I called upon God to help liberate me and my children. They must accuse God for he did the fighting. They think me a very bad man. Father, all I have done in my life has been to procure a living for my children and my old parents and to save them from the dangers of death."

In the first place The Bull was not present when Custer was vanquished. In the second place he was well aware of all the facts of the battle after two years; would not have authorised the publication of an article with so many defects in it. In the third place The Bull and everyone else knew that until Reno opened his attack the Indians had no idea that white soldiers were in the valley, with the exception of the few warriors and hunters who had seen them in the vicinity of Crow's Nest. The crowning prevarication by the unknown correspondent: his statement that The Bull knew three days in advance Custer was coming. The Indians held an all-night social and cermonial dance the 24th-25th; something they would never have done had they known they were about to be attacked. The squaws and children did not attempt to get away until after Reno attacked. Finally, this fabric of prevarication is ridiculous; had the hostiles known soldiers were coming they could have ambushed them in a hundred places before they ever got close to the villages — and they would have for Indians fought most valiantly in defence of their homes and families. In conclusion, the dateline itself is suspicious for at that time The Bull was at Woody Mountain up in Canada, well aware that Americans wanted nothing so much as to get their hands on him; he was avoiding Americans with every wile at his command.

It was articles and stories like this one which the white people believed after news of Custer's passing spread. The illiterate Indian had no way of combating them — if he had cared to. But the truth was — and remains — that those stories did irrevocable harm; the Indians were branded liars as well as fiends. More detrimental however, was the resultant controversion of facts which, through deliberate distortion, obscured the truth. After eighty-three years and twice that number of liars the story of the Battle of the Little Bighorn remains the most controversial page in American history. The Indian warriors had achieved a triumph over an enemy they had every reason to wish dead. Washita and the campaign of 1873-74 had taught the Sioux and Cheyennes to hate Custer. They had designed a special war-honour to be awarded the warrior who killed him. This was a willow circlet with a scalp stretched within it. In the centre, on the flesh-side of the scalp, was painted a red hand and a black heart. But this award was never given for even after they knew who they had killed, the hostiles were never satisfied about who had fired the shot. In fact the identification of Custer was delayed while the squaws and warriors rode over the field taking clothing, personal effects, and weapons. As incredible as it may seem quite a few of the Indians had never before seen white men; others who had seen them, had never touched one before, nor been close to them. Being curious these people now strolled among the corpses.

White Bull had injured his ankle during the fight earlier and it was swollen. While he remained upon his horse he had no trouble but when he dismounted he could not re-mount. He was riding over the field looking for a pair of leggings he had removed before the battle when he came upon Bad Juice near a clump of brush where the leggings were. Bad Juice waited until White Bull had retrieved his leggings then helped him to re-mount and together they rode aimlessly, seeking trophies. White Bull saw a fine fringed jacket with brass buttons lying in the dust near a blond soldier. He got down and picked it up. Bad Juice also dismounted and White Bull showed him some papers which were in a pocket. Bad Juice had known a lot of soldiers; had spent some time at Fort Abraham Lincoln. He went over where a naked soldier lay and bent down to look at his face. There was a bullethole in the corpse's left breast and another — with powderburns — in his left temple. The soldier was calm looking, as though he had died in his sleep. Most of the dead soldiers' faces were twisted and contorted; this man's was not and Bad Juice recognised him. He told White Bull: "That one there was Long Hair Custer."

White Bull was only slightly impressed. He and Bad Juice told others Long Hair Custer had probably been the soldier-officer commanding the invaders.

A little later two Indian women, Mahwissa and Monaseetah, walked among the bodies too. Monaseetah's little son was Yellow Bird, whose grandfather, Monaseetah's father, had been killed in the fighting. The women approached a naked white man beside whom squatted a Sioux warrior in the act of cutting off the soldier's trigger-finger. The young squaw made a cry and the warrior looked up. It was Monaseetah; she was staring at the body of Custer — the father of her son Yellow Bird.

But there were disputes over which soldier had been the leader. Captain Tom Custer also wore fringed buckskin, as did Charley Reynolds. When the warriors stripped the colonel's brother they found tattoos on his body. One in particular intrigued them; an eagle with outspread wings on his chest. Someone lanced the eagle counting coup upon it. An Indian boy found a round object attached to a gold chain. Thinking it to be strong white-man medicine he wore it around his neck and for a day or so it made a ticking sound, then it became quiet. He had never seen a timepiece before.

Custer was not scalped. Those favouring the belief he shot himself point to this for proof; Indians did not scalp people who committed suicide. More practically, Custer was not scalped because his thinning hair was valueless as a scalp; anyone displaying such a mousey trophy would be derided. Additionally, there were innumerable scalps of much better quality on the field. If he *had* shot himself only a few would have witnessed it; others, not knowing, might have taken his hair; that they didn't gives strength to the other tale of why he was not scalped.

After sundown those still hacking at the bodies returned to the camps. Word had spread of the coming of more soldiers. Aside from the new threat it was not good to stay where the smell of death was increasing every hour. The bands prepared to strike their camps and leave the valley. There was some difficulty rounding up the trophy seekers and squaws, pilfering and mutilating the dead. Reno's men having fallen closer to the village received most of this attention. Little boys strolled among the bodies firing arrows into them. A large number of extremities had been hacked off. Later identification was made doubly difficult by beheading. Squaws who had lost fathers, brothers, husbands, sons, in the fighting, slashed the bodies mercilessly. Others removed genitals in the belief such talismen increased the fertility of the tribe. Knives and hatchets were used in this work. Two little girls had the head of a 'Ree which they carried back to camp between them, each holding a braided pigtail. Their mother was aghast; she was part Arikari, Bloody Knife had been her half-brother. Another head which aroused considerable interest was that of a soldier with gold teeth.

While the camps were being struck there was much visiting. A warrior had a small object with a tiny arrow inside it which always pointed north. This was thought to be especially powerful medicine; he was offered many horses for it but declined. The guidons which had been taken were correctly assumed to be the particular flags of soldier-companies. Custer's personal battleflag was accorded honour as the soldier-chief's private symbol of great medicine. A Cheyenne, Yellow Weasel, found a bugle. He and all his friends tried to blow it; when they could make no noise come out they decided it was broken. Yellow Weasel kept it and after a while was able to make loud noises with it. The Sioux had also found a trumpet. With better success they made such a racket the men on Reno's Hill at first thought there were soldiers down across the river.

Sitting Bull was angered at the elation of the Indians who appeared more concerned with plundering and trading than in leaving a spot where the gasses let off by dead and bloated men and horses made the night unpleasant. Eventually he was instrumental in getting the Hunkpapas to erect burial scaffolds for the dead. The Cheyennes put their dead upon horse-drawn travois and took them out into the night to places where they would not be found; crevices, caves or unsuccessful in finding these, they buried them upon ground and piled stones over them.

The Sioux painted their dead warriors' faces bright colours, dressed them in their finest clothing and lashed them to burial scaffolds looking upwards. Special lodges were designated as burial tipis. One such lodge held twenty corpses side by side. By far the greatest burial ceremony was held for Lame White Man, the Cheyenne chieftain. His family mourned all night long, his body was followed into the night by a large party of friends, all wailing and gashing themselves.

As the night hours drew out the men on Reno's ridge began to suffer for water. They could hear the wailing of the Indians, see their movements around the hundreds of campfires; some thought it would be safe to slip down to the river and fill canteens. Going down in small parties these soldiers would progress very cautiously for they knew there were "wolves" hiding around the hill. They had to cross open ground to get to the water. Some made it, some did not. Iron Hawk shot a soldier who was filling canteens. When the soldier threshed about in the water Iron Hawk ran forward and beat him to death.

Atop the ridge the friendlies Hairy Moccasin, White Man Runs Him, and Goes Ahead decided to try and escape. It was their belief the Sioux would return at dawn and kill the rest of the soldiers. White Swan could not go because of his wounds. The three Crows disappeared in the darkness. Later they saw a Sioux warrior riding a grey horse and leading a mule. Goes Ahead slipped up and killed the Sioux, took his scalp and gave the horse to White Man Runs Him. The mule had gotten away in the mêlée, now the three Indians took turns riding the grey horse and trotting along beside him. They progressed in a northwesterly direction keeping to the trees as much as possible, until they were all around the hostile encampment.

Lieutenant Varnum, evidently thinking as the escaped Crows had, that the command would be overwhelmed come daylight, held a council with the remaining scouts. The Crows, White Swan and Goose, being wounded, were to stay with the soldiers under the care of Half Yellow Face, but the Arikaris under Forked Horn were to try and get past the hostiles and reach Terry's column. Each was to take the identical message, an account of what had happened up to now, and the location of Reno's ridge. Goose then insisted he too should go along. Varnum agreed; he also sent along a white soldier, a sergeant. Mounted upon horses from which the shoes had been removed the fugitives got as far as the river. They were travelling in a body. Sioux "wolves" fired upon them. Goose and Young Hawk returned the fire then all fled back up the hill. The white soldier told Lieutenant Varnum it was no use. Varnum agreed.

But the Crows who had left earlier got up close to a camp of friendlies shortly before dawn and called out. The other Crows, believing it was a Sioux attack, charged them. All the shouting they did was unavailing and Goes Ahead shot two horses from under their riders before he could make his people believe the new arrivals were Crows, not hostiles. They reported what they knew and what they imagined, which included a tale that by now the other Crows and soldiers had been killed on Reno's hill. This occasioned a great outburst of wailing. Squaws who thought they were widows — including Half Yellow Face's wife — gave away their horses and slashed their arms, legs, and breasts.

Back at the hostile encampment there was intermittent gunfire. Many of the Indians slept, but a lot of them did not; aside from the howls of those in mourning there were a number who had gotten drunk on plundered whisky and shot up the camps and the surrounding underbrush. The "wolves" keeping watch on Reno's command fired up the hill from time to time to let the soldiers know they were surrounded and could not escape. Once, there was a terrible fright. Someone cried out that soldiers were attacking the village. Warriors rolled out of their sleeping robes and ran for their horses, women and old people began to wail, children to scream. Then it was seen that a party of young warriors had dressed themselves as soldiers and emulated a close-order advance upon the encampment. There was much acid comment upon this joke; the warriors went grumblingly back to bed but most of the people had had too great a fright for sleep. These sat around talking, making up victory-chants, resuming the trading in soldier-goods which had enlivened the evening before.

It began to rain. Not much, just enough to settle the dust. The Indians got their robes and sat around the fires awaiting daylight. Women were striking the lodges; it was 26th June, 1876; the tribes would break up, go their separate ways as soon as it was light enough to see. More soldiers were coming. This was also a dead-man camp. There were a great many bitter relatives of those who had died or been killed who were against moving; they advocated fighting the approaching soldiers, killing them too; then wiping out the men in the defensive circle across the river. Most of the people however had had enough fighting. They were content with the victory they had, sought no other and wanted now to continue the hunt. Arguments continued until daybreak and meanwhile the squaws dismantled the tipis, caught up the travois-horses and packed them. There was a brisk barter in cartridges. The Indians had gathered up about ten thousand rounds, more ammunition than they had ever had before. This was of course pointed up as another reason why they should all stay together and fight; it was not sufficient reason; more important was the fact that with so many bullets a great number of buffalo could be killed. These were much more valuable than dead soldiers, which could not be eaten.

But hours before a grief-maddened squaw had indeed butchered a soldier, dressed him out like a deer or an antelope and cooked him. But no one would eat the meat, not even the squaw herself, although many admitted it smelt and looked appetising enough.

Chapter Four

IN after years Curly the Crow wrote a little book describing his "escape" from the battle. According to this version he had fought with Custer until it was evident the hostiles would triumph, then he let his hair down, disguised himself as a Sioux with stolen clothing, slipped through the ring of Sioux and Cheyennes, caught a loose horse and made his way to the Yellowstone River where he hailed the captain of the supply ship *Far West* and told him of the disaster which had overtaken the 7th Cavalry and Colonel Custer. This story was accredited for a long time but subsequently it was turned up that Curly, while enrolled as a scout, may not have been in the battle at all, that it was entirely possible that he did not leave the hillside to participate in the fighting. This belief was prevalent among his surviving tribesmen as well as the hostiles.

For obvious reasons the hostile warriors did not publicly renounce Curly. They discussed the battle only among themselves. It was many years before they would believe the government's promise of amnesty and re-enact what had happened, and by that time all the principal leaders were dead along with most of the warriors.

But, before dawn on the 26th the dead had been sent on their way, the wounded made as comfortable as possible on travoises, the lodges taken down and all preparations for leaving the valley completed. (It is the author's belief that with the departure and separation of the tribes the last chance to integrate knowledge of casualties was for ever lost; many of the leaders and warriors never met again.) By this time every camp had heard of the approach of another soldier-column. Some strong-hearts wished to go back and fight Reno's men but others were anxious to get out of the valley. As soon as it was light enough to see some of the bands began trailing out of the valley. White Cow Bull had acquired a rifle in the previous fighting. He went to a hill which overlooked the soldier-circle and began sniping with it. Bows and carbines did not have the range to reach the white men that the rifle did. One soldier arose to his knees to remove his greatcoat and White Cow Bull shot him. Another soldier had the heel shot off his boot. The dug-in defenders then ascertained White Cow Bull's position and began firing at it but their carbines did not have the range. White Cow Bull took his time. As the sun climbed, became hotter, he saw a soldier break out of the circle and try to run down to the river. He fired at the man and missed. A "wolf" hidden in some underbrush closer to the running man shot and killed him. Although the soldiers were suffering for water, the cries of their wounded audible; no more tried to get down to the river.

The strong-hearts were reinforced by others from across the river as the morning wore on. From atop their hill the soldiers could see the Indians straggling out of the valley in every direction, but the warriors around them seemed determined to force a fight. They finally congregated on the south slope where the ground was chewed up from the previous days' fighting and launched a frontal attack. There was no cover for the Indians and the soldiers — with twenty-five thousand rounds of ammunition from the packtrain — poured volleys of shot into them. A few reached the ridge. One Sioux actually got close enough to the defenders to reach over their saddle- and bread-box barricade with his coup stick and strike a dead soldier for a particularly daring coup. When he turned to run back down the hill a soldier shot and killed him. This was the Sansarc, Long Robe.

The roar of gunfire brought other warriors riding back towards the ridge but Sitting Bull was anxious about the soldiers his spies reported were drawing close to the valley. He ordered the fighting to stop. "If we kill all of them," he told the warriors, "a bigger army will come against us. Let them go." An Oglala called Knife Chief was talking with some warriors about this when a soldier got to his knees behind the barricade atop the ridge, aimed carefully and shot Knife Chief through the body. A great howl went up from the Oglalas. They carried the wounded man with them and retired.

By this time nearly all the lodges were down and packed. From his vantage post atop the hill Major Reno looked down upon the confusion of the camp and said, "I think we are fighting all the Sioux Nation, and also all the desperadoes, renegades, half-breeds and squawmen between the Missouri and the Arkansas and east of the Rocky Mountains." His implication that white men and half-bloods were fighting against soldiers was not unique. On the 25th when his men had heard the bugles being blown they had at first thought it might be relief. When this had not materialised it was rumoured that white deserters were with the Indians. It is not known to be true but it is not impossible that squaw-men *were* with the Indians; half-bloods most certainly were. Additionally, the great variety of clothing among the hostiles could have belonged to deserters, desperadoes, Indians, in fact anyone. There were the usual rumours in later years that white renegades had indeed been with the hostiles; it is entirely plausible that they were. The dead which were found upon the field afterwards were exclusively Indian, but in their approach to the field Gibbon's column (the one under hostile surveillance) came across several Indian graves and burial scaffolds. These were not violated to ascertain whether they contained dead Indians or whites.

Spies brought word that the new soldier-column, which had passed the night at the mouth of the Little Bighorn River some twelve miles away, was now marching up-river. It did not make very good time because it was made up largely of infantry.

Sioux warriors Many Lice and White Bull rode downriver to look at this new force. When they were satisfied with what they saw they made a charge upon the pack-train, succeeded in cutting out seven or eight laden horses and drove them away. In spite of pursuit they escaped and returned to the encampment. By the time they got back there were only a few lodges still standing; the last and largest gathering of free Indians upon the plains was scattering to the four winds. Many Lice and White Bull drove their captured horses with them and followed the trail of their band.

To Reno's thirst-tortured men the departure of the Indians lent hope which many refused to accept as proof of relief. They had watched the warriors along their front withdraw. Had seen the lodge coverings pulled down, the naked poles lashed upon horses for travois runners, the warriors cavorting a-horseback amid the confusion and racket, the great show of activity and energy, without daring to hope. A few die-hard warriors clung to the underbrush and covert until middle afternoon, firing and yelling taunts, but gradually they left, went splashing back across the river to join the departing bands. The Battle of the Little Bighorn was over. In order to integrate what happened next it is necessary to go back several days before the battle, to General Alfred Terry's column. (The Indians knew him as *Wicanpi Yamini.*)

He was travelling blind; still did not know Crook had been defeated on the Rosebud or that Custer was a day and a half in advance of schedule in approaching the valley. In order to affect a juncture, at least with the advance units of the other columns he sent a strong detachment of volunteers a hundred miles across Indiandom seeking Custer's camp. He thought he knew about where Custer would be and believed if he were able to ascertain the location with some accuracy he would be able to close the circle with both Crook and Custer so as to meet both expeditions when the Indians were sighted. Custer was supposedly across the Yellowstone which was high country where snow-water run-offs made whitewater in mid-summer. Some Crows with his detached scouting unit were drowned. Several soldiers were also lost in the fordings but the remainder of the volunteers of H and F Companies eventually got to the uplands where they rode far and wide without finding Custer. They returned to Terry's main column and reported their lack of success, General Terry had misgivings. The volunteers had just put their mounts on the picket-line when Officers' Call was sounded. Terry held a brief conference then ordered General Call sounded and the command given for the advance. The volunteers had enjoyed one cup of coffee, four hardtacks and one pipeful in thirty-six hours; they were understandably irritable.

General Terry rode with Captain Ball of H Company in the van. He sent scouts ahead under Lieutenant Bradley. They rode down a long, beautiful valley under a clear and sparkling sun. Nearby was a swollen creek screened with the usual willow growth. It meandered down the valley until it disappeared from sight in a slot in the foothills. Down this slot was straggling a dusty disarray of Indians. Many of these had uniforms on. Some had sabres — taken from Crook on the Rosebud, and in earlier battles; the 7th Cavalry did not have sabres on the Little Bighorn.

General Terry ordered a halt. The Indians also stopped. Terry ordered Lieutenant Roe of F Company to take some enlisted men and ride ahead to determine who the Indians were. In the ranks it was thought the Indians might be some of Custer's Crows and 'Rees. Roe loped ahead with his escort. The balance of the command lounged in their saddles waiting. They were shocked out of lassitude when the Indians fired upon Roe, who immediately turned back. General Terry ordered the horses lariated behind dismounted soldiers. Horse-guards were detached, the soldiers told to lie down and prepare for battle, and the Gatling guns which Custer had refused to take with him were brought up from the rear. Also, three pieces of artillery.

While Terry was making ready for battle the Indians had not moved. From well beyond carbine and pistol range they sat their horses watching. Their error in underestimating Terry's firepower was demonstrated when he ordered the artillery to open up.

The Indians broke when shells burst among them, fled in every direction. When silence settled again General Terry ordered the advance resumed. His march down the valley, the skirmish and subsequent delay in getting underway again had used up most of the day, 25th June, 1876. The column bivouaced at the mouth of the river and resumed the advance the following day. Some warriors burst out of the willows and stampeded several horses from the pack-train; the rear-guard was doubled, additional scouts sent on ahead. Several miles farther down the valley the column was halted in the open where a brace of poles had been set into the ground with a thong stretched between them. Hanging from the thong were three severed heads of white soldiers. That was the foretaste. . . . It was the morning of the 26th.

Lieutenant Bradley of Gibbon's command was ranging far ahead in charge of Terry's scouts. He was the first white man upon the Little Bighorn battlefield after the Indians withdrew. His specific instructions were to seek and find Colonel Custer. He did.

His first meeting was with scavenging Indians who fled upon sight of him and left behind their personal effects. His scouts recognised the things left behind as Crow property and Bradley signalled for the Indians to come back. This they declined to do until satisfied Bradley was a white man instead of a Sioux or Cheyenne in soldier apparel. The Crows turned out to be some of "Mitch" Bouyer's scouts. They told Bradley what had happened. Stunned, he at first did not believe them, but ordered a courier back to Terry with the news then proceeded towards the spot the Crows said he would find Custer's five companies. The first thing he saw upon approaching the northernmost area where the hostile village had been was a dead cavalry horse.

When General Terry received the courier from Lieutenant Bradley he likewise evinced disbelief but notwithstanding ordered a fast advance. It was clear some kind of an action had taken place.

It was late afternoon, 26th June, after making a cautious advance, that Lieutenant Bradley went into bivouac determined to await the main commands' arrival. He was not more than ten miles from Reno's ridge where the survivors of the fight were enjoying their first respite after forty-two hours.

Before dawn on the 27th the combined command proceeded its winding way down the Little Bighorn Valley again. Lieutenant Bradley was out with his scouts. He crossed the river and topped out upon a slight rib of land and not far off saw a great scattering of "white things" upon a sidehill. Pushing on he came upon Custer's battlefield.

The dead men were naked and mutilated, in a great many instances they were unrecognisable. All were bloated. Bradley halted his scouts and sent word back to Terry.

Far away and overhead Reno's command was still maintaining the defensive circle. The afternoon before they had watched the Indians moving westward. Until the 27th they had not dared stand up with field-glasses and study the size of the abandoned village; four miles long and a half mile wide, they now estimated its size to be not less than twelve thousand Indians. Reno's officers returned to the circle where enlisted men were digging graves. Eighteen dead men within the circle had to be buried; fifty-two wounded at long last got water to drink. The stench was becoming overpowering. It was ordered that their bivouac be moved where the air was less contaminated.

Early morning the 27th sentinels reported a large dustcloud coming into the valley from the direction the Indians had taken. Soldiers walked to the edge of the ridge to see. It was said the Indians were returning. Major Reno dispatched Lieutenants Hare and Wallace across the river to reconnoitre; it was rumoured Custer was at last approaching.

Hare and Wallace identified the advancing men as soldiers. At about the same time the men on the ridge ascertained this from the way the columns were formed. (Colonel Gibbon's command was in advance of Terry's column.) Lieutenants Hare and Wallace were overcome, set their mounts into a run and did not draw rein until several officers ahead of the column veered off to intercept them. Escorted to General Terry the first question asked was: "Where is Colonel Custer?" Terry had Bradley's second message. As the troops rode towards Reno's ridge he told Hare and Wallace what Bradley had reported.

Reno's men reacted in various ways to deliverance. It was recorded that some of the men sat down upon the ground after the relief arrived and looked out over the valley; others wept. Some talked, others listened; all were stunned at the news of Custer's vanquishment. Lieutenant Bradley rode back to Reno's ridge. After noon he was directed to take Captain Benteen and several others where Custer lay. This second visit to the battlefield turned up the only survivor found on the field; Comanche, the horse of Captain Keogh. He was wounded and apathetic, the saddle hung under his belly. After this identification visit General Terry also visited the field. It was reliably reported by those near him that he stood above Custer and said: "That's what you get for disobeying orders, God damn you!"

The bodies had been greatly abused by the Indians. In after years the Northern Cheyenne Wooden Leg recalled: "I went . . . to the grounds where we killed all of the soldiers. Lots of the women and boys were there. The boys were going about making coups by stabbing or shooting arrows into the dead men. Some of the bodies had many arrows sticking into them. Many hands and feet had been taken off," (Cheyenne custom was to remove a fallen foe's fingers; they wore necklaces of these trophies: Author) "and the limbs and bodies and heads had many stabs and slashes. Some of this had been done before by the warriors, during and immediately after the battle. More was added, though, by enraged and weeping women relatives of the Sioux and Cheyennes who had been killed. The women used sheath knives and hatchets."

The dead were not all where they had fallen. Some lay alone, others were in groups. Where Custer lay was one of the largest groups. The flight from the ford was marked with men and horses. The number of dead was in excess of two hundred. Years afterward when he was a General, Edward S. Godfrey said that according to his count two days after the fight there were two hundred and twelve corpses. Another authority said that among the bodies were several who were never identified and doubt existed whether they had participated in the fight. These men were headless; it seems unbelievable the Indians would have brought other victims to the field and left them. Captain Keogh's religious medallion worn around the neck had been taken out and laid upon his chest. His body was not mutilated. Several officers and men were never identified, were listed as "missing". By the time burial details were set to work the bodies had lain naked in the sun for three summer days. There was much reluctance on the part of grave details to seek additional bodies.

There was reason for a while to believe that one soldier might have escaped. Friendlies and later the hostiles accredited this story, but after the passing of several decades without his re-appearance he has been generally believed to have been slain. ("Survivors" of the "Custer Massacre" did quite frequently come forward; none were ever recognised.) A soldier who was said to have escaped into some trees may have survived the fight, but in all probability he was wounded and later perished; at any rate he was never identified and did not come forward to identify himself. It is not impossible that he was killed by friendlies after the battle. The matter of survivors would continue to annoy historians and Army Records personnel for years.

The day prior to the burials, 27th June, 1876, the first of an endless barrage of contradictions which has lasted eighty-three years, began. The 7th Infantry's Lieutenant Bradley, Terry's chief-of-scouts during the advance into the valley, added his bit by writing the Helena, Montana, *Herald* a month after the battle, 25th July, 1876: "In the presence of so great a disaster as that which overtook the regular troops on the Little Horn, (sic) and the consequent excited state of the public mind," he said, "and its eagerness to get hold of every detail, however minute, of that unfortunate affair, it is to be expected that many stories of a sensational character, having no foundation in the truth, would obtain with the public. Of such character is that now going the rounds of the press to the effect that the Sioux removed Custer's heart from his body and danced around it, a story related upon the authority of one Rain-In-The-Face, a Sioux chief, who participated in the fight and afterward returned to the agency. Of the same character also, is the sweeping statement as to the general shocking mutilation of the bodies of the soldiers who fell on that occasion. The bare truth is painful enough to the relatives and friends of those unfortunate men without the cruel and gratuitous exaggeration of their grief that must come from the belief that they had been horribly mutilated after death. . . . In my capacity as commandant of scouts accompanying General (Colonel) Gibbon's column, I was usually in advance of all his movements, and chanced to be upon the morning of the 27th June, when the column was moving upon the supposed Indian village in the Little Horn Valley. I was scouting the hills some two or three miles to the left of the column itself, when the body of a horse attracted our attention to the field of Custer's fight, and hastening in that direction the appalling sight was revealed to us, of his (Custer's) entire command in the embrace of death. This was the first discovery of the field, and the first hasty count made of the slain resulting in the finding of 197 bodies reported to General Terry. Later in the day I was sent to guide Colonel (Captain) Benteen to the field, and was a witness to his recognition of the remains of Custer. . . . Of the 206 bodies buried on the field, there were very few that I did not see, and beyond scalping, in possibly a majority of cases, there was little mutilation. Many of the bodies were not even scalped, and in the comparatively few cases of disfiguration, it appeared to me the result of a blow with a knife, hatchet, or war-club to finish (off) the wounded man, than deliberate mutilation. . . . The bodies were nearly all stripped. . . . The real mutilation occurred in the case of Reno's men, who had fallen nearer the village. These had been visited by the squaws and children and in some instances the bodies had been frightfully butchered. Fortunately not many were exposed to this fate."

Lieutenant James H. Bradley, first white man upon the battlefield after the Indian withdrawal, said rather emphatically that most of the dead soldiers were *not* mutilated, except closer to the Hunkpapa village where Reno's casualties had fallen. The warrior who had fleshed-off Lieutenant Cooke's elegant sideburns and who had actively participated in both battles, at opposite ends of the encampment, said they *were* mutilated; that the squaws and children had hacked and defiled the bodies indiscriminately and relentlessly. The question would not be resolved by an inclusion of statements of those on both sides which alternately said the dead had been violated, or had not been violated. In context they only agreed upon one point; that Reno's men had received the worst treatment. Otherwise the contradictions were at odds and endless. The men detailed to bury the dead should have known; so should the Indians who had nothing to gain — and much to lose — by admitting butchery.

Pictorial evidence would have lent irrefutable substance to one claim or the other, and some years back such a reproduction did appear in the possession of a man in Pierre, South Dakota. Its clarity was sufficient in every detail to show a Model 1894 Winchester carbine lying in the foreground, to the astonishment of those who knew such a weapon was not manufactured in 1876. Such substantiating marvels line the corridor of research with prevarications.

Perhaps the *degree* of mutilation should be discussed. It was common practice among Plains Indians to put out the eyes of fallen foemen so that they could not see to pursue Indian spirits in the Hereafter; it was also common to cut the Achilles tendon, to lift the hair and remove trigger-fingers. These were customary; scarcely a white man found after an Indian fight was not so treated. White soldiers understood these things, why they were done; they expected to find comrades handled in this manner. They did not especially regard such totems as mutilation. On the other hand disembowelling corpses *was* classified as mutilation — Tom Custer was disembowelled. Hacking off heads, arms, legs, genitals, was considered mutilation. If these things did not happen as Lieutenant Bradley said, why did the burial details list so many of the fallen as "unknown" and "unidentified?"

Dismemberment of a body was mutilation but the removal of a scalp was not; who established or even adhered to a code of ethics respecting what degree of butchery constituted mutilation? The Indians had one belief, the soldiers another, civilians and newspapermen yet another. The dispute was incapable of settlement and so remains. ". . . Beyond scalping," Lieutenant Bradley said, implying scalping was a normal thing, a common and accepted thing, ". . . there was very little mutilation."

Burial details were sent out on the 28th. It was impossible for several reasons for decent burials to be afforded. The ground was like iron, the implements for digging make-shift; adequate for making a bivouac but unsuitable to mass interment of corpses which had been lying in the sun for three days. The soldiers wore handkerchiefs over their faces soaked with mint, but even with this they could not stand the stench for more than a few minutes at a time. The weather was swelteringly hot. Graves were rarely deeper than eight or ten inches. In many cases the bodies were pushed or rolled into a narrow indentation, dirt was thrown over them and brush was then piled over whatever protruded.

The graves were dug close to where the

bodies lay. The heat, the odour, the un-pleasantness contributed to a general dis-tastefulness which inspired the burial parties to complete the job as soon as possible. After the relief column left, coy-otes and other scavengers exhumed a great many of the corpses.

The combined commands of General Terry and Colonel Gibbon numbered ap-proximately one thousand men. Major Reno's force including Benteen's detach-ment, McDougall's company and the pack-train, was roughly three hundred strong. In addition the reinforced columns had ordnance. This was one column; the War Department was soon to make up others as strong and stronger. News of Custer's defeat aroused the nation but it would take time to marshal troops and post them to the Northwest and meanwhile the Indians fought skirmishes but in general avoided battle in order to fill their larders against encroaching winter.

The land was vast, thousands of Indians in hunting parties could lose themselves in it with little effort. Predicting their course was impossible; the Indians themselves did not know where they might be from week to week. They were following game. The chieftains wanted a great cache of food laid by. They knew that ultimately their people would have to go into the reservations and when they did there would be reprisals; starvation was what they expected. There was good reason — and past experience — to indicate they might expect little else. Sitting Bull heard from friendlies that escape into Canada would offer security. He undertook the journey and after arrival was informed by Canadian authorities he might live in peace so long as he did not violate the law.

Other bands went westward, to the age-old hunting grounds of their people. The hostiles scattered in many directions and meanwhile fresh troops and greater weapons arrived in the Northwest. Forts and cantonments were enlarged. Strong patrols scouted for hostiles. Some were found and fought. There were innumerable little skirmishes, a few pitched battles, but it wasn't until an encampment of Minniconjous, Brûlés and Oglalas were located at Slim Buttes in Dakota Territory by a powerful army that a great battle was fought.

The Sioux were outnumbered; in no position to offer resistance. Their village had not been established in such a fashion to permit a careful watch to be maintained. They were in fact trying to hide, not seek an enemy, and in consequence were down in a big coulee when Fred Grouard, a scout from Captain Anson Mills's company of General Crook's command, located them.

This was the 7th of September, 1876. The Indian village was under *Wasicun Tasunka* — American Horse; a close friend of the Oglala Crazy Horse. Grouard carried word to Captain Mills of his discovery. Mills moved forward in the night and struck American Horse's village at dawn. The Indians were caught unprepared. Although outnumbered they put up a stiff and stubborn fight. Mills could make no headway and dispatched a courier to General Crook with news that he had a large hostile village at bay. General Crook hastened up with the balance of his force, numbering two thousand effectives. There was a lull in the battle. The Indians had been driven back into the rocks beyond their village. Crook sent them a demand for surrender. American Horse replied saying General Crook would have to come and get him. The fighting was resumed. As casualties mounted on both sides Crook became convinced the hostiles meant to die fighting. He sent another demand for surrender.

For a long time there was no reply then a warrior called out the Indians would give up. The squaws came out of hiding first. They were chanting a song of mourning, many were injured, nearly all had blood on them. Next came the surviving warriors. Several of them were supporting an Indian whose teeth were locked around a piece of wood; it was American Horse. A bullet had struck him in the stomach in such a manner as to rip his belly open. Only by holding his blanket tightly around his midriff were his entrails prevented from falling out. When the warriors put him down upon the ground he sat there rocking back and forth for a while, then he toppled over dead.

General Crook had his vengeance for the defeat at the Rosebud. He had the vanquished hostiles lined up, women and children in the lead, warriors last. There were exactly twenty-eight survivors. He surrounded them with nearly two thousand soldiers and marched them into captivity.

Just before American Horse's people were taken away a strong war-party appeared on the bluffs above their village. These were warriors under Crazy Horse. They sat motionless watching their comrades being marched away. They made no effort to succour them. Later, Crazy Horse fled westward with his band — and a few survivors from American Horse's camp which had managed to reach his village — and established a camp on the Tongue River.

But while the Indian wars were being prosecuted to their end, the last reverberations of the Custer affair were not yet over. General Terry said: "I do not tell you this to cast any reflection on Custer . . . but I felt that our plan must have been successful had it been carried out. . . ." Newspapers vied with one another in accusing those connected with the Battle of the Little Bighorn of all manner of failure, dereliction of duty, and even cowardice. Everyone from the Crow and Arikari scouts down to the horse-holders was castigated without mercy, and naturally the two ranking officers came in for scathing denunciation. Their reactions were different; were in fact essentially the reaction of men altogether different in personality and character.

Marcus Reno was sensitive; he was popular with his soldiers, somewhat of an admirer of women, not a teetotaller; generous and warm by nature. Whether these were attributes essential or even desirable in a soldier would be questioned.

Everything he did on 25th June, 1876, came up for study and scrutiny. Several things damned him; one was his confusion in the woods, his panicked flight towards the river. Another was his agitation after Benteen came up. Still another was the way he pressed himself upon the ground and refused to move when Benteen told him they must charge the Indians, force them back from the ridge or be overwhelmed. His record as an officer during the Civil War was in his favour, but the general opinion of his conduct on the Little Bighorn was against him. National opinion condemned him. The men who had fought under him felt differently; a week or so after the battle they sent the following petition to Washington:

"Camp near Bighorn on
Yellowstone River,
July 5, 1876.

To his
Excellency the President
and the Honourable
Representatives of
the United States.

Gentlemen:
We the enlisted men the survivors of the battle on the Heights of the Little Horn River, on the 25th and 26th of June, 1876, of the 7th Regiment of Cavalry who subscribe our names to this petition, most earnestly solicit the President and the Representatives of our Country, that the vacancies among the Commissioned Officers of our Regiment . . . be filled by the Officers of the Regiment only. That Major M. A. Reno, be our Lieutenant-Colonel, vice Custer, killed; Captain F. W. Benteen our Major, vice Reno, promoted. The other vacancies to be filled by officers of the Regiment by seniority. . . ."

To this petition — denied by General Sherman who did not show it to the President — was attached the signatures of two hundred and sixty-three enlisted men, survivors of the Battle of the Little Bighorn. An angry letter to Wyoming's congressman W. W. Corlett from Fred Whitaker, Custer's biographer and champion, demanded a court of inquiry be convened to examine the conduct of both Reno and Benteen. This was done 18th May, 1878, upon Reno's solicitation. However, by the time the court was called the statute of limitations placed Reno beyond the threat of army court martial dismissal. There were many who pointed this up as an attempt on Reno's part to escape punishment. The transcript makes excruciatingly dull reading, but in it are the words of others who were with Reno. Lieutenant Hare said: "If Reno had continued to advance mounted (against the village; before his flight across the river), I don't think he would have gotten a man through: the column could not have lasted five minutes. His dismounting and deploying us was all that saved us."

Captain Myles Moylan said: "In my judgement if he had continued to charge down the valley he would be there yet." Lieutenant Charles C. De Rudio who had been abandoned in the woods said: "I saw no indication of cowardice on Reno's part; nor any want of skill in handling and disposition of the men. When he halted and dismounted I said, 'Good for you,' because I saw that if we had gone five hundred yards further we would have been butchered."

Speaking of their stand in the timber Lieutenant Varnum said: ". . . I don't think we had enough men to hold it and keep the Indians out. . . ." Lieutenant Hare again: "Major Reno stayed in the timber until all hope of support from Custer had vanished . . . I can only estimate his conduct by the way it turned out. I think his action saved what was left of the regiment." Lieutenant Edgerly said that Reno was excited but calmed down after reaching the hill: ". . . By then he was perfectly cool but by no means heroic." Lieutenant Godfrey concurred, he said Reno suffered from "nervous timidity . . ." Brevet Colonel Benteen said he did not consider Reno cowardly.

The Court of Inquiry absolved Marcus Reno and his fellow-officers of dereliction of duty or cowardice. Reno's continuance in the service was not long. A haunted and sensitive man, dishonour came finally in the most humiliating fashion. He was apprehended drunk and peering into the bedroom of a fellow-officer's wife's quarters one night and dismissed from the service.

Captain Frederick W. Benteen weathered the storm better. A reserved, burly man, with eyes like moist stones, whose detestation of Custer was reasonably clear, Captain Benteen's courage and coolness, if not his bluntness and scorn for diplomacy, left him nearly unassailable. His Civil War record was consistent with his nature; it was not outstanding but it mirrored plodding determination and thorough bravery. He was a fighter but not a reckless one; he had no great aspirations such as had goaded George Custer, and neither was his personality as vacillating, as unpredictable. He was strong-willed and cool-headed and no aspersions against his conduct on 25th June would stand up in the light of inquiry and the knowledge of the man. He was known to have a flashing temper and a devotion to duty second to none in the army. Those who attacked him could not honestly accuse him of cowardice, indecision or imprudence. His disposition did nothing to endear him to soldiers or civilians, but as a conscientious frontier officer he was known to have no peer. The Court of Inquiry cleared him as it had cleared Reno and others. The findings were reviewed by the President and confirmed.

Meanwhile the campaign of attrition went on. In November diminutive but ferocious Ronald McKenzie struck the Cheyenne village of Dull Knife at Willow Creek, in Montana. Dull Knife's people had not participated in the Battle of the Little Bighorn; it made no difference. They were conquered in a swift fight. Two Moon surrendered without a fight and for his part in Custer's disaster was deported with all his people to a reservation where an unexpected — and contentious — honour was bestowed upon him. The Government appointed him principal chieftain of the Northern Cheyennes. Little Wolf and Dull Knife when taken with their bands, were less fortunate. They were sent to Indian Territory (Oklahoma). Three years afterwards they broke away from the reservation and made a heroic fifteen hundred mile flight back to their homeland. By that time public sentiment had changed sufficiently to reward their suffering and courage with an amnesty; they were permitted to remain with their relatives in the Northwest.

On 8th January, 1877, while in bivouac, General Nelson Miles was surprised by a powerful war-party which appeared on the bluffs overlooking his camp. The soldiers were just finishing their morning meal when a warrior called down in perfect English: "You have eaten your last breakfast!" The Indians then charged Miles' camp. This was a band of warriors under Crazy Horse.

General Miles directed the artillery brought up and fired against the Indians. The result was devastating. In addition soldiers got into the rocks overlooking the warriors and poured a lethal fire into them. It began to snow and General Miles had his artillery brought up closer and fired repeatedly. The Indians fled and Miles did not pursue them.

Crazy Horse was one of the last defectors to "come in". Antiquated Red Cloud was induced by the Army to go find the Oglala and his band and convince them only death awaited those who persisted in defiance. Red Cloud found the hostiles and sent back the following note to an Army officer:

Sir My Dear. I have met some Indians on the road and thare say the Indians on bear lodge creek on 16 april and I thought let you know it. And I think I will let you know after I get to camp so I sent the young man with this letter he have been to the camps before his name is arme blown off.
RED CLOUD

When Red Cloud found Crazy Horse the hostiles were in pitiful condition. Their horses were dying of starvation and the people were no better off. There was a lot of talk but in the end Crazy Horse agreed to come in.

The Red Cloud Agency was brimming with Indians. There was much discontent and distrust. The Army did much to foster a division of the Indians. Red Cloud was said to be a tool of the whites; he was villified for his part in Crazy Horse's surrender, but on the other hand Crazy Horse was looked up to for he had not surrendered unconditionally like Little Chief of the Cheyennes and Two Moon; he had exacted terms from the soldier-chieftain which included the right to go hunting when he wished. Crazy Horse was the focal point of all the dissidents; it was imperative that he be reconciled to his lot or killed, for as time went on Indian restlessness became acute, the distrust grew and factionalism prospered. The Army and Indian Bureau considered a new outbreak very likely. But the soul was taken out of the Indians when Crazy Horse, ordered imprisoned and struggling in the arms of soldiers, was run through by a bayonet in the hands of a red-headed soldier of the Ninth Infantry. He died in anguish the night of 7th September, 1877, eight months and one day after his attack upon General Miles; his last big attack.

Not long before Crazy Horse's passing the Blackfeet Sioux chieftain Kill Eagle whom Sitting Bull had particularly encouraged in the attack upon Reno and Custer, was imprisoned at the Standing Rock Indian Agency. The renowned Man Of War White Bull was humiliated by being forced to return his horses and weapons acquired at the Little Bighorn. Crow King and Gall, more tractable, were permitted to go unmolested. Old Red Cloud, blind and senile, was induced to sign a treaty with the Government ceding the sacred Black Hills to the United States.

The Army tried repeatedly to get Sitting Bull to come down out of Canada. He would not; would stay there until 1881. Bobtail Horse took service with the United States Government, and because he was known to be close to The Bull he was sent north to prevail against The Bull's inhibitions. Nothing came of their reunion; Bobtail Horse returned without Sitting Bull. But in mid-summer, 1881, Sitting Bull's little band was hungry. It was a bad hunting-year in Canada. He led his people to Fort Buford and surrendered to the Army. Five years had elapsed since Custer's blunder. Eighty-seven Sioux were with The Bull, all that had stayed with him at the end. They were sent to agencies, the Bull to the Missouri River compound where he lived disconsolately until William F. Cody — "Buffalo Bill" — recruited him for a touring Wild West show. Rain In The Face was among Cody's exhibition Indians. Showmanship undertook to build up the parts played in Custer's defeat by these two Indians. Rain In The Face was said to have eaten Custer's heart raw, Sitting Bull to have planned the "strategy" which had overwhelmed Custer.

Sitting Bull's travels with Cody's show had sanguine effects upon the old chieftain. He saw how other Americans lived; insisted Indians should be permitted the same freedom of movement and the right to congregate, to worship as they pleased. When the Ghost Dance craze came northward from Nevada — where it was started by a Piute named Wavoka — Sitting Bull denounced the Army's edicts forbidding the Sioux from participating in its ceremonials and dances. Succinctly the Ghost Dancers believed that a great storm was coming which would cover all the white people, and even the Indians who were not dancing when it arrived. After the storm passed the world would be as it had been before any white people had come; the Indians' old way of life would be preserved and returned to them. The buffalo, which had vanished under the relentless slaughter of hide-hunters between the seventies and late eighties, would also return.

This pathetic "religion" found great swarms of converts among the Northern Cheyennes and Sioux. What happened was a sad, a tragic thing. Prohibited from staging these dances the Indians persisted. Soldiers were sent to break up the gatherings. Sitting Bull denounced governmental interference. He was an official of the religion — not a real believer so much as a disciple who wished with all his soul such a thing was possible. The thousands of white settlers in former Indian country appealed to the Army for protection. Clearly the Ghost Dance cults were exciting the Indians anew. When the Army moved reinforcements to the agency posts Sitting Bull's anger reached a zenith. It was then decided he should be killed and accordingly the man who was to do it was Crow Dog, who had also been at the Little Bighorn.

About the time of The Bull's murder the 7th Cavalry got revenge on Wounded Knee Creek in South Dakota, where a band of Indians under Big Foot — Minniconjous — were attacked without warning and slaughtered. The casualties numbered an appropriate two hundred and twenty dead Sioux — but many were women and children.

Last of the Little Bighorn's survivors died not long ago. Lieutenant Varnum passed on in 1935, Sitting Bull's son John, a deaf-mute, in 1955, Iron Hail also in 1955. *Henala* . . . Enough . . . The phantoms leave us on dusty horses, their equipment making a distant clank . . . the flash of sunlight on a great Sioux bonnet, a lance with scalp-coups moving in the wind. Lieutenant Donald McIntosh's notebook was taken from a captured warrior with a bullethole through it. Fortunate Mohawk-Indian McIntosh, killed so swiftly.

Varnum, driving captive hostiles ahead saw something shining on the blanket of a squaw; "Benny" Hodgeson's watch with the workings removed; the spidery inscription on the inside of the back-cover commemorating a graduation from West Point. Varnum retrieved it, sent it to Hodgeson's father. All the pathos of an era threading its way softly through the dry and impersonal pages of history; all the sadness and the memories.

Lieutenant Algernon Smith's ornate watch-fob with its little golden horse taken from another Indian and carried by his close friend Lieutenant "Gib" Gibson until he died. A note from Elizabeth Custer saying she thought she would return to Monroe, Michigan, for a while but that she would never forget the 7th Cavalry.

Lieutenant Cooke's matchless sidewhiskers made into a handsome scalp-circle by a squaw and kept, oiled and brushed, until she died. Trooper Tanner's topknot buried at Fort Meade by soldiers who did not know whose head it had come from; knew only that they had taken it from a warrior and that it was a white-man's scalp.

Mollie McIntosh, buxom and dominating,

and with a great wish for social acceptance, collapsing when she heard from a half-drunk friendly that her husband was no more.

Busy hands of army protagonists working in conjunction with fertile imaginations to create a hero where none existed; Custer's body taken east in great style to be re-interred among the nation's great and fallen.

Letters from the East in endless procession asking how "he" died and Indians sitting in the dirt remembering a great gathering, a great time of hunting and trading and rejoicing. Newspapers denouncing Reno's losses — fifty-six killed, fifty-nine wounded; denouncing in a guarded way the power which permitted a command to be defeated at such cost — fifty-one per cent lost; hinting of treachery among the officers.

Colonel Sturgis, detached commander of the 7th Cavalry receiving word of the death of his son; the death of George Custer; the death of a black man he had known as a woodcutter at the post and some-time interpreter.

And of all Curly the Crow's tales one that could be verified. When he arrived on the banks of the Yellowstone three crewmen from the *Far West* saw him but could not understand his sign-talk and sent him closer to the steamer. He boarded the ship and was given a meal. He talked while gorging himself. A squawman and interpreter named George Morgan listened and repeated. Others stood still in amazement. Curly was then seventeen years old, a handsome if somewhat dark Indian. He said he had not taken part in the fight; had only lingered long enough to be sure of the outcome then had raced for the Yellowstone. The other stories would emerge later. Still later, when Reno's wounded began arriving in litters, Custer's body also came aboard.

Hairy Moccasin, Goes Ahead and White Man Runs Him, who had seen Custer fall before fleeing were discredited for their subsequent defection from Reno's hill. It was many years before their tales were heeded and by then Curly had been to Washington and lionised as the "sole survivor of Custer's Last Stand".

Mysteriously Crow and Shoshoni friendlies with Crook a hundred miles away told the white soldier that Custer and his men had been killed the evening of the day they sat down with him. Crook could not believe they could know such a thing if it had happened, which he did not believe. Queried as to how they acquired this strange piece of information while fighting was still in progress on the Little Bighorn, the friendlies declined to say.

Two friendlies rode to Fort Abraham Lincoln with the story that Custer was dead; that he had shot himself. They said this within the hearing of Elizabeth Custer. Bradley's story that Custer was not mutilated — and the Army's shipment of the body in a sealed casket — added to the mystery.

"The Custer Massacre" became saleable copy to every printer and publisher in America. That Custer's defeat was no massacre made no difference. A "massacre" occurred only when the fallen were attacked and vanquished without warning; were killed without defending themselves. The 7th Cavalry went to its death fighting with everything available; carbines, pistols, knives, fists; they were beaten in fair combat upon grounds and terms of their own choosing. They were defeated by superior numbers, by equal courage — by faulty leadership — *but they were not massacred.*

Custer was buried at West Point and a legend emerged, fed by lachrymose writers for nearly a hundred years. An adulating populace recalled "Custer's luck". A less appreciative Colonel Sturgis said: "Custer's 'luck' has backfired." In high places there was silence, but once Grant spoke briefly and bluntly: "I regard Custer's massacre as an unnecessary sacrifice of troops brought on by Custer himself."

The part played by The Bull Who Sits Among Us has been unnecessarily confused by historians. Many claim The Bull was miles away when the Battle of the Little Bighorn was fought; others say The Bull was not a great Hunkpapa chieftain — which in fact he was not; he was a medicine-man, something altogether different from a war-leader or hereditary chieftain. In addition, for the edification of those interested, there was an Oglala with the same name who achieved some prominence among the Sioux. Although he died several months before the Custer battle much that he did in earlier years has been accredited to the Hunkpapa Sitting Bull. As a matter of fact the name "Sitting Bull" along with its variations was a comparatively common one among the Sioux. Instances of misinformation are not confined to modern writers, for when General Crook met a band of Northern Cheyennes on the Tongue River under Little Hawk, and fought them, he claimed the result as "a smashing victory over the Sioux under Crazy Horse". This was shortly before his final defeat on the Rosebud; he had not yet met the Sioux.

Little by little civilian probing disclosed that Colonel Custer had been specifically directed by General Terry not to break the agreed-upon marching schedule. Army efforts to white-wash its martyr were in part successful but could not muzzle the newspapers or the civilians. The result was a dispute which gathered strength as the years passed. It was said Marcus Reno was drunk on the 25th; that Alfred Terry told Custer before his departure from the Yellowstone, to be careful, to do nothing reckless and await the rest of the command.

Why did Weir attempt to lead Edgerly and his company away from the ridge? Because, it was said, he had heard a volley fired southward; the signal among troops in the field seeking succour. And after The Bull was shot to death — where was he buried? The Indian policemen who killed him and were themselves killed in the fight, were buried with honours; The Bull was buried secretly, no one knew where he lay; there was no marker.

And Benteen — why didn't he hasten to Custer's aid? He received the message telling him to "Be quick. Bring packs," but he did not make haste and Custer went to his death. Benteen was not the hasty type; he was no Custer who dashed into battle with an orderly riding at his side with his personal banner. Benteen was colourless but he was also prudent. He differed from Custer in this; that's why he survived the Little Bighorn and Custer did not. But why did he not obey Custer's order? For the same reason he disobeyed his other order, the one telling him to march "over into the next valley" and the next, and the next; because he had no faith in Custer and because he owed a great responsibility to the men he led.

How was it that some of the Indians had Martin-Henry repeating rifles? Some were smuggled weapons traded by unscrupulous whites, many were not. It was the custom to reward Indians with presentation pieces; it had been the custom for a hundred years. But Martin-Henrys were very few; until after Reno fled across the river the Indians were not well armed with any kind of gun.

The greatest argument arose over whether Custer did or did not violate his orders. He obviously disobeyed them in the spirit of their meaning; he knew he did. Terry and Gibbon understood what was to be done perfectly. So did Crook; the difference was simply that Crook was prohibited from co-operating by a battle. The written context of Custer's orders were ambiguous; actually senseless, but behind them lay Alfred Terry's misgivings. He wished to impress upon a man whom he knew to be insubordinate, the great need for good sense and caution. "Now Custer," he had said, "don't be greedy but wait for us." And Custer had waved his hand and said: "No, I will not." And afterwards Gibbon wrote: ". . . Perhaps we were expecting too much to antici-

215

pate a forbearance on his part which would have rendered a co-operation of the two columns practicable."

But Custer did not know how many Indians he was going against. But he *did* know. Two months before he was killed on the Little Bighorn he sent Charley Reynolds on a reconnoitre through Indiandom. This was 1st April, 1876. Reynolds was to locate the Indians, appraise their movements, numbers, and disposition. When he returned Reynolds reported to Custer that "from three hundred to six hundred lodges under Sitting Bull are now en route to Berthold." Moreover, Phil Sheridan wired Fort Abraham Lincoln, 14th May, 1876, more than a month before the battle: "It is represented that they have fifteen hundred lodges, are confident and intend to make a stand." General Terry knew also, for as early as 24th March, 1876, he had wired Sheridan: "The most trustworthy scout on the Missouri recently in hostile camp reports not less than two thousand lodges and that the Indians are loaded down with ammunition."

Custer knew how strong the Indians were; knew also their temper. In the face of this knowledge he divided his command and attacked. He may have thought the Indians would flee but Charley Reynolds had said they would not; so had Sheridan. What possible reason did he have for what he did? Glory? Honour? Ambition? Yes; all three reasons; he was "Custer of the 7th" the "boy general", the slighted egotist with Presidential aspirations. What did he accomplish? Broken hearts, tragedy too deep for tears, orphans, widows, ghosts in dirty blue standing vigil in a lonely valley where nothing has changed; nothing been added but stone markers. Tragedy painted in bold strokes upon the pages of a nation's history. Truth robbed of its starkness by historians who have gentled the facts, moulded a tissue of prevarications and doubts, kept opprobrium and guilt from the shoulders of a man who has emerged a hero — although he was not a hero.

So ends a tale of history — and other damned lies.

Lauran Paine who, under his own name and various pseudonyms has written over 900 books, was born in Duluth, Minnesota, a descendant of the Revolutionary War patriot and author, Thomas Paine. His family moved to California when he was at an early age and his apprenticeship as a Western writer came about through the years he spent in the livestock trade, rodeos, and even motion pictures where he served as an extra because of his expert horsemanship in several films starring movie cowboy Johnny Mack Brown. In the late 1930s, Paine trapped wild horses in northern Arizona and even, for a time, worked as a professional farrier. Paine came to know the Old West through the eyes of many who had been born in the previous century and he learned that Western life had been very different from the way it was portrayed on the screen. "I knew men who had killed other men," he later recalled. "But they were the exceptions. Prior to and during the Depression, people were just too busy eking out an existence to indulge in Saturday-night brawls." He served in the U.S. Navy in the Second World War and began writing for Western pulp magazines following his discharge. It is interesting to note that all of his earliest novels (written under his own name and the pseudonym Mark Carrel) were published in the British market and he soon had as strong a following in that country as in the United States. Paine's Western fiction is characterized by strong plots, authenticity, an apparently effortless ability to construct situation and character, and a preference for building his stories upon a solid foundation of historical fact. ADOBE EMPIRE (1956), one of his best novels, is a fictionalized account of the last twenty years in the life of trader William Bent and, in an off-trail way, has a melancholy, bittersweet texture that is not easily forgotten. MOON PRAIRIE (1950), first published in the United States in 1994, is a memorable story set during the mountain man period of the frontier. In later novels such as THE HOMESTEADERS (1986) or THE OPEN RANGE MEN (1990), he showed that the special magic and power of his stories and characters had only matured along with his basic themes of changing times, changing attitudes, learning from experience, respecting nature, and the yearning for a simpler, more moderate way of life.